HOW TO BE A CORPORATE QUEEN

HOW TO NEGOTIATE YOUR SALARY, CAREER CHANGE, AND LIFE TO ACHIEVE EVERYTHING YOU'VE EVER WANTED

ASHLEY NAUMANN

ONYX PUBLISHING

First published in 2020 by Onyx Publishing, an entrepreneurial imprint of Notebook Publishing of Notebook Group Limited, 20–22 Wenlock Road, London, N1 7GU

www.notebookpublishing.com

ISBN: 9781913206437

A CIP catalogue record for this book is available from the British Library.

Typeset by Notebook Publishing.

To all the women that were told they could never make it in a "man's world".

And:

To my Dad (#DanTheMan), who told me I'd always make it in a "man's world". Love you.

WELCOME TO THE START OF YOUR FOREVER

HAVE YOU EVER WANTED SOMETHING so badly, with all your heart and mind, and yet you couldn't figure out how to achieve it? This might be the next promotion; the dream career; that raise you've always wanted.

Well, now is the time to take it! No more sitting on the side-lines and waiting for destiny to grab you by the hand, because over the next 150 pages or so, I'm going to take you on a journey that is going to transform not only how you look at promotions and raises, but how you see yourself and your life.

As you go through this book, have a pen and paper ready: you can't transform unless you act, and, in line with this, this book is filled with lots of quizzes, charts, and helpful guides to keep you moving in the right direction.

Get ready! Here we go.

ABOUT THE AUTHOR

ASHLEY NAUMANN IS THE ORIGINAL Corporate Queen, the CEO of Beauty and a Boss, a pricing and sales strategist extraordinaire, a real estate investor, powerlifter, and puppy mom to the wonderful majestic Merlin—all under the age of 30! She has lived on both US coasts, started a real estate and insurance business from the ground up, and moved through the corporate ranks at Fortune 500 companies in big pharma, big tech, and big finance like a shark after blood. She has also been overweight, underpaid, and has had zero sense of self-worth more times than she can count.

But she grew; she became stronger; she owned her power.

And, conveniently, she now brings her knowledge to you!

Her journey now consists of travel and fun, as well as her true passion: helping women to understand their value and the power of pricing and negotiating! Through her life, she has encountered workplace harassment, discrimination, and prejudice, all of which requiring her to grow—not only as a person, but as a businesswoman; to learn the ins and outs of the industries she was serving (male-dominated, to say the least!); to learn how to be the best; to learn how to overcome and beat the system. Because, let's face it, everyone can talk until they are blue in the face about workplace discrimination and prejudice—but until you start standing up for yourself, *nothing* is going to change for you. She challenges you to read this book with that concept in mind: that unless you do the work; unless you plan; unless you take action; nothing will change.

This book isn't a sob story or a woe-is-me novel. Indeed, as much as this path isn't an easy one, if you truly want to reach your full potential, you've come to the right place. Ashley is excited to release this first version, especially targeting corporate women looking to advance in their careers and become that Corporate Queen!

And, if you're determined to kick start your career even faster: accelerate your journey by taking a look at some of the additional high-value trainings and other extras Ashley has carefully put together for you to aid and enhance your path, available below:

https://beautyandaboss.clickfunnels.com/joinus

SECTION 1:

THE PREWORK

CHAPTER 1:
WHAT DO I REALLY WANT?
IS BEING A CORPORATE
QUEEN MY PATH?

YOU'RE STUCK IN A JOB you hate, or at least one that underutilizes your mind. It takes too much time. The kids/dog/boyfriend/your sanity are all out living their lives, and you're stuck at work. It's draining, and it's definitely not what you want out of your life.

Or maybe it is—but not in this capacity. Maybe you love your job, but you don't make enough to support all your efforts. You feel undervalued, and you are not being supported in reaching your true potential.

Sound familiar? This is all-too-common for women across the country who are torn between being #PowerWomen and #LivingTheirBestLife, but are stuck in a situation where the means don't justify the ends.

So, let's take a look at what we've got so far:

You: Unhappy

Life: Passing you by...

But *why*?

"Why" is always an interesting question; I've found, over the course of my life, that I only ask "why" when I didn't get what I wanted and I was feeling sorry for myself, since "why" justifies that I did what I was supposed to do, but didn't take the right actions.

1. Why did I fail my first business?
2. Why did I go into debt?
3. Why did I stay at a job that I hated?

None of these questions leads to productive responses; rather, they lead to one answer to one question, with no change in behavior. So, we are instead going to start this journey by asking "what" (and eventually "how") instead of "why".

1. What do I hate about my day-to-day job? (How can I fix it?)
2. What do I want to change in my life? (How can I change it?)
3. What do I see myself doing in 10 years? (How do I get there?)

Before we can jump into problem-solving and negotiating for something, you have to know *what* your end goal is. Is it a new job? A promotion? More time off? Job flexibility?

QUIZ

Start by asking yourself these questions:

1. Do you hate getting ready for work on Sunday?
2. Do you get anxious or nervous going to work after a break?
3. Do you feel drained after your day at the office?
4. Do you long for those three-day weekends or time off?

If you answered "yes" to more than two of those questions, it sounds like this job is not an ideal fit. Is this because your boss is terrible, or is the job just not stimulating enough? Are you paid fairly for what you do? Are you undervalued? Be specific. Don't forget, we are trying to change your life here!

So, *what* makes you unhappy at your current job? Fill in as much as necessary.

I am currently unhappy at work because...

_____

_____

_____

_____

_____

_____

_____

_____

_____

_____

_____

_____

_____

_____

_____

_____

_____

_____

_____

_____

_____

_____

_____

Responses typically fall into a few categories here:

1. You hate your boss (but don't hate the work);
2. You're underpaid;
3. You're under-stimulated;
4. You actually dislike the work that you're doing;
5. You like the work and your employer/employees, but have problems with the work environment;
6. You feel trapped—financially or otherwise.

If you're unsure, just keep taking the quizzes, and we will sort it out.

If you already know which one applies to you, however, head straight to the quiz that matches best with your circumstance.

If your boss is the problem but you like the job, sounds like it's time to send out some resumes.

1. Do you hate your boss?
2. Do you dread going into the office on Monday?
3. What is your favorite thing about work?
4. What is your least favorite thing?

SWOT IT OUT!

As you will see throughout the book, "SWOT It Out" means to review the strengths and weaknesses of an argument to come to an informed conclusion.

When we SWOT It Out, we are referring to identifying our Strengths, Weaknesses, Opportunities, and Threats. (These latter two elements, however, will be discussed as we select your ideal goals, so let's just focus on the Strengths and Weaknesses aspects for now!)

In this case, write a list below of all the strengths of your boss and all the weaknesses, and then do the same for your position. See the examples in Row One.

Strengths of My Boss	Strengths of My Position	Weaknesses of My Boss	Weaknesses of My Position
Timely	Flexible work schedule	Bad temper	Boss micromanages me

Now, compare the lists. Is Column One or Column Two longer? Is Column One or Column Three longer? Is Column Two or Column Four longer?

If One > Two, your boss may not be perfect, but is actually better than the job. Keep assessing below. If, however, Two > One, then your boss is probably the problem. Resume- or job-change time!

If One > Three, then your boss has more strengths than weaknesses. The problem isn't your boss! Move onto the next quiz. If, however, Three > One, then your boss is the problem in your eyes. Resume- or job-change time!

If Two > Four, then you enjoy your job. Further, if One > Two, then it sounds like your job and the boss are not the problem: time to search for deeper meaning. If Two or Three > One, time to send out those resumes!

If your boss is okay but the job is under-stimulating, sounds like a career change might be in order. Time for some real soul-searching! We'll touch on this in a bit.

QUIZ

If your job is okay and the boss is okay, but you're still not happy, continue here:

1. Do you feel overqualified for your position?
2. Do you feel underpaid for your position/workload?
3. Does your manager support your professional development?
4. Do you have the necessary flexibility at work required for you to support your lifestyle?
5. Do you have performance reviews (with review of compensation) at least once a year?
6. Do you have measurable goals to show progression within your position?

If you answered "yes" to #1, *how* are you overqualified?

_____

_____

_____

_____

_____

_____

If you can clearly articulate *how* you are overqualified and you like your job, it's time to consider a promotion; move down to the Path to Promotion section!

If you answered "yes" to #2, *what* is the appropriate pay for your workload?

_____

_____

_____

How did you come up with that figure?

_____

_____

_____

_____

_____

_____

Did you also answer "yes" to both #5 and #6?

_____

_____

_____

_____

_____

All of these will be crucially important as we discuss how to negotiate a raise. Skip to Raising The Bar below.

If you answered "no" to #4, *what* would the ideal working scenario look like to you?

_____

_____

_____

_____

_____

_____

Does your job allow for such working conditions?
(i.e. a daycare assistant can't work remotely.)

_____

_____

_____

_____

_____

_____

If yes, then it's resume time! Continue to Review That Resume below. If no, then continue as you were.

If you answered "no" to #1 and #2 and have made it this far, welcome to the world of personal reflection! This means that:

It's not your boss,
It's not the job,
It's not the pay.
It's *you*.

CHAPTER 2:
REVIEW THAT RESUME

S O, YOU'VE COME TO THE conclusion that it's time to make a career move: different company; different job; something else entirely.

First things first, pull out your resume and take a look at the format, previous job descriptions, accomplishments, and updates. When was the last time you updated your resume? And when was the last time you did any research on resumes?

Now, due to the technological age being in full effect, I recommend a full resume review. You can pay a corporate consultant in your area to review and provide feedback; however, whether you're going to do that or not, I highly recommend going through the following steps yourself:

Pretend your resume doesn't have your name on it and look at it as if it's someone else's that you've never met. You have 30 seconds to do so.

What does your resume say about this person? Are they neat? Is it organized? Do their previous experience (titles) align with the new job they're applying for? Are their credentials clearly listed somewhere? Is their name, phone number, and email spelled correctly and easily seen?

These are just a few basic items you want to make sure you have absolutely clear:

1. That your name, phone, and email are spelled correctly and are easily legible.

2. Your credentials are clearly listed (e.g., if you're looking for a new nursing position and don't have your R.N. listed, that's a problem; if you're a Salesforce Admin and don't have the certification listed, that's a problem).

3. Your recent job history. If your resume is from 10 years ago, it will seem as though you haven't progressed or grown as a career person since. Even if you are in the same role, you've had to have learned some new skills, right?

4. Everything fits on one page. Unless you've been in the workforce for over 20 years, your resume should only be one page long. I've talked to hundreds of recruiters, and it is very unlikely that anyone will ever look at the second page of your resume—so why have it?

5. Spelling and grammar. Both should be 100% correct. There is no excuse for this.

6. Last but definitely not least, your resume should be accurate. Lying on your resume will not get you anywhere; most companies are using online HR software that can see fraud a mile away. Those same companies will also run background checks on your education and job history. I'm not saying not to embellish or describe things effectively to meet the job criteria, but don't lie.

Now, to the more complicated task: as you're reviewing your resume, what does it convey? Does it support the job you're looking to get, or one of inferiority? If you're going for a "reach" position (a.k.a., something that is above your current standing), are you reflecting skills that show you are prepared and capable of holding such a position, or are you simply recapping what you've done over the last 10 years? Remember, this is your time to shine; don't shy away from accomplishments and accolades; don't leave off certifications and degrees. Mention anything that is relevant to the position.

When reviewing, check to make sure your statements are action statements, with purpose. This should include *what* you did and *how* it helped.

For example, take the current version:

Ran analytics for management and learned problem-solving methodology.

Does that show that you *added* value? How did you help anyone? This is really just a summation of the things that you did, as well as the skills that you learned to help yourself—and, as a matter of fact, we don't actually have any evidence you learned anything; just that you witnessed it, without any connection to the specifics.

Try this instead:

Decreased executive portfolio analytics development and delivery time by 81% through use of Tool X, Tool Y, and Buzzword Skill methodology.

In the new version, I have not only noted exactly what I did, but *how* I did it. This demonstrates that I learned a skill *and* applied it to help the company. This also shows my executive interaction skills, tool knowledge, and evidence of "soft skills". My work actually *did* something; I didn't just talk about it.

The final step in resume reviewal is to review job postings: look at the jobs you would like to apply for and save their websites for later.

Do the skills you've now clearly articulated match the job postings you're looking for? Are you using the current buzzwords that LinkedIn and Indeed are using to describe the positions you want? This is a common way to help get through the HR nightmare that is an online application: if someone is looking for a Corporate Engagement Officer, your resume should mention "Corporate Engagement Officer"— even if, in reality, that is a fancy way to say HR event planner, and that was your last role title. Use the words your industry is using; that way, you can instantly be at the top of the pile.

Bonus step: Have a friend or family member review your resume for spelling and grammatical mistakes. It's easy to overlook something that you've reviewed 100 times, but a careless error could be seen in seconds. Ask them if you were looking to apply for a new job, what would they think of your resume? This will give you an outside opinion *without* having to pay a resume specialist.

On that note, if you're going to hire a resume specialist, make sure to pull real references for that person. Look online for XYZ Company reviews (and make sure the URL is not related to that company!) and look up bad reviews for XYZ Resume Service. This will give you a good idea of what you're dealing with. If you are switching industries, I highly recommend working with a resume specialist in your market and in your desired field, as this will help you to craft your resume in line with what your future employers are looking for, using the skills you've gained in a different direction. Don't be discouraged if you don't have everything at first glance; many skills are transferrable! You'll just have to think outside the box in terms of how to word them. Remember: frame your resume as if you are the perfect candidate for the position. Make sure your resume specialist knows you are coming from a different industry and can help frame you in the light you want to be seen. Don't let your experience go to waste!

As a last note, you may want to have different copies of your resume highlighting different sets of skills that you have if you are applying to a variety of roles (e.g., if you are looking for a Corporate Recruiter position, but are also open to other HR opportunities, you may want a version specifically highlighting your recruiting talents and contract negotiation, and another version that discusses HR policy review, legal compliance, and HR software skills). Remember, the online system is very tricky, so you'll need to make sure your resume is getting seen and is keyword-specific to each job, as this greatly raises your chances!

CHAPTER 3:
RAISING THE BAR

S O, YOU'VE DECIDED THAT YOU like your job and that you want to stay, but you're underpaid. What do you do?

This is a classic problem many women face, as our biological nature is to nurture: we nurture our relationships; we nurture our coworkers; we nurture the amount of work we are given. This also leads to over-nurturing. Let me explain...

Have you ever taken on a project when you already have too much work going on?

And have you ever said yes to something just because of who the person is, without considering the time restraints and whether it is something that's within your job scope?

Do you just say yes because you're afraid to say no?

This is what I like to call "scope creep" or "job expansion"—and not in the positive way concerning career growth and development! Rather, this is when people see you as a "yes" person, which, in some cases, can be great—but then it allows the powerful to take advantage of your willingness to help by piling more and more work on top of you. In the end, you are doing three peoples' jobs instead of just your own; you're over-nurturing your coworkers/boss/management and undervaluing your time.

This leads to emotions such as resentment, fatigue, and stress—just to name a few.

If you find yourself in this situation, but do, indeed, like your job, it's time to determine your outcome.

Do you want a raise? Or do you simply want to do less work so that the value matches your effort?

This is an important distinction, since you can often do both—but not always. Prioritize which is more important so that you can take the proper steps to get there. Make sure you also take into account your personality; I'm a Type A person, so simply doing less to match my salary isn't an option for me. Would you be okay doing less because it's fair? Or would you rather just be paid more?

You'll likely find it useful to go through the below steps alongside the additional training (available exclusively for you at https://beautyandaboss.clickfunnels.com/joinus). This will really allow you to get a better idea of the bigger picture we're painting here.

If you simply want to do less work to match the efforts of the salary and position you have, follow the three simple steps below. Notice, I didn't say *easy*; just because they are simple doesn't mean they're easy! It takes guts and courage to reprioritize and stand up for what you deserve. You're doing this to better your life! So, let's begin:

1. Set Boundaries
When you come and go should be set in stone: if you're not required to answer emails outside of working hours, don't! If

you're not supposed to be working on weekends or on your days off, *stop*. And I mean actually stop; not hypothetically. Just *stop*. Be firm with your boundaries and your time. People need to take you seriously; otherwise, you compromise on your word and your integrity, as well as your courage and resilience. Set calendar office hours and do not accept, review, read, follow-up... *anything* outside of those working hours. I personally liked to set my available hours from 9am–4pm, 8am–9am and 4pm–5pm being blocked every day on my calendar to be used for catching up on emails, having guaranteed working time (not meeting time), or even the occasional summer happy hour—because everyone knows that you deserve it! After 5pm, I'm out of the office—and, once 7pm hits, my out-of-office would come on, saying that I would respond within one business day, starting at 8am the following morning. What a relief it was to know that I could go to the gym every day at 7pm, and didn't have to worry about the stress of needing to respond to something!

Now, you try:

What is your daily working timeslot?

_____

_____

_____

_____

_____

_____

What is your daily working, but meeting-free, timeslot?

_____

_____

_____

_____

_____

_____

What is your daily non-working timeslot (a.k.a., free time)?

_____

_____

_____

_____

_____

Now, onto Step 2.

2. Implement

Explain your boundaries when asked. This is a new change, so when you don't respond on Saturday evening or on Wednesday at 10pm to something that is a non-emergency, someone is definitely going to bring it up—and even if they don't, you can confront the situation head-on proactively to show your newfound strength and alignment. Address the situation head-on with a saying like the one below, which can be included in an out-of-office alert after your standard working hours:

"After 7pm is non-working time for me, and unless there is a true emergency, I am totally disconnecting to be with my family and friends. This is best for my wellbeing, as well as my being able to ensure that I can be at my absolute best when I am working, as I'm sure you can understand. I will absolutely address your concern at the earliest available time during working hours. Thank you and have a wonderful evening."

This statement shows that you care about yourself *and* your position, and also explains that you are giving 110% when you're at work, and not allowing you this time off would be detrimental to your working attitude and mental health. Furthermore, by using the term "non-working", you are immediately clarifying that you should not be working right now, which automatically eliminates any room for HR nonsense (e.g., "Oh, you're out drinking"; "Oh, you're picking up your kids every day and cutting out"; etc.). They do not need to know what you're doing: this time is your own! Don't explain what you are doing in your free time; it is none of their business. Typically, you won't need to post this for very long; people's behaviors tend to change quickly when they realize you have boundaries set and are sticking with them.

Just as a warning from personal experience before we progress: this may bring up other flags. Your boss may want to speak to you as to why you posted this, or they may even send it to HR, since you mentioned your wellbeing. Don't despair: you're doing the right thing! Courage, my friend; stand up for your email and your time. The email is in no way disrespectful or rude; it is simply setting boundaries. If your boss wants you to be on the clock 24/7 and brings that up (i.e., the old, "Really, Sheila, I don't think that email was necessary"), stay the course and say to him/her exactly what you wrote in the email: "I need this for my wellbeing and work/life balance." If they push back again, say that you're happy to discuss advancement opportunities or pay increases to match the level of effort that is now required for the position—and watch how quickly their tune changes! If they insist, however, it may be that your boss is, indeed, deliberately taking advantage of you, and, in this situation, you should be looking for alternative employment. Keep a positive attitude and mindset. Remember, you decided to embark on this journey to benefit yourself and your family. Don't forget your "why"!

And, last but not least...

3. Say No

When you have too much to work on, say no; when it's outside of your frame of work, say no; *before* you're up to your eyes in backlog, say no. You deserve to have a reasonable workload, and if they expect more out of you than is humanly possible, they either need to pay up or "GTFO", as I like to say! They can hire someone else.

Many people worry that this mentality will get them fired, but I've found that this is rarely the case: typically, when an employee is overworked, it is because the boss and teammates think they can get away with doing less, or the company itself is strapped and doesn't want to hire another employee when you're there and will do all the work for them. When you stand up for yourself, however, you are not only setting boundaries for yourself and your wellbeing, but also for them as a team—as well as guidelines for the relevant roles and responsibilities per pay level. The risk with this strategy is that you will most likely not be seen in a great light in terms of a raise or a promotion; however, your original goal was only to do the work you are fairly paid for.

Now, you may say, "Well, I don't want to just do the basics; I want to outwork, outperform, and get paid for it!"

First off, good for you! Welcome to controlling your destiny in Corporate America.

Second, buckle up, buttercup! It's time to make a plan.

And yes, all of this should come *way* before you try to negotiate for a dollar.

So, you want to get a raise; this is the first step to controlling your future and preparing for the path to promotion. You need to start by assessing where you are within your position, pay grade, and pay market. Write answers for the following questions to help define what realm is possible for your first raise. In the long-term, any raise is possible, but if you've started low in your pay bracket, it will take time to reverse and bring your correct payscale back in balance.

Current Situation

What is your current salary?

_____

_____

_____

What are your benefits and what is their dollar value? (This should include a percentage for bonus, retirement match, commission if applicable, and stock options.)

_____

_____

_____

_____

_____

How long have you been at the pay you are at currently?

_____

_____

_____

Are raises distributed based on merit, or time? Are reviews given at regular intervals?

_____

_____

_____

Did you negotiate your pay when you started, or at your last performance review?

_____

_____

_____

Are you due for a raise within a year?

_____

_____

_____

Market Situation

What is the current market unemployment rate? Is the job market considered to be weak or strong?

_____

_____

_____

Is your field in high demand? (This can be found by searching your job title in Google and seeing how many results you receive. The more, the higher the demand.)

_____

_____

_____

What is the average pay for your position? What is the range (high/low)? (Take a look at Glassdoor or LinkedIn or the BLS [Bureau of Labor Statistics] for ideas of ranges in your current market.)

_____

_____

_____

What are the average benefits packages for other companies similar to yours?

_____

_____

_____

Based on the above factors, it is time to compare where you currently are versus where you could be. Is your current salary within the common range for the same position? If it is below or within, then there is a much higher likelihood for negotiation in terms of getting a raise. If, however, you are currently above the standard salary band, don't despair! You can absolutely still earn a raise; your setup will just need to be more detailed and merit-focused.

When comparing salaries, don't forget to take a look at bonus packages (from what you can find) and stock options, flexible working environments, and other additional benefits (i.e., childcare help, etc.). Many companies are using these benefits in addition to raising salaries, so you need to factor this into your salary review, too.

Give yourself a score from 1–10 in terms of where you land on the average salary score (e.g., if you have an average salary but don't get to work from home, you would be rated a 3; or, if you have a below-average salary but get to work from home and have vacation plans and stock options, then you may weigh your salary closer to a 6, or even 7).

Regardless of the score, this is only a starting point. It's not necessarily better to have a super low score, as this can create a challenge when negotiating. Further, you may be at a company that doesn't value their employees, or you may have grossly undervalued yourself when you earned the position (don't despair—we can fix this!). Of course, it is also not impossible to get a raise with a high score, since high scores typically demonstrate a company that develops their employees and understands the market conditions. However, you do still need to understand where you stand.

If you have a score under 4:

You may be working for a company that does not value their employees, or you may have undervalued yourself during your interviewing and original negotiation. There is more room for improvement here, but you need to temper your expectations. If the company does not value their employees, you may need to seek employment elsewhere so as to be properly paid. Saying this, if you didn't negotiate during the interview and happened to be at the bottom of the salary curve, the following steps should drastically increase your professional value, potentially leading to a dramatic increase in salary.

If you have a score between 4 and 7:

This is the most common situation for most employees, including myself when I first started negotiations for a raise! Most employers do not want to drastically underpay their corporate employees, as they know they will be farmed away to another company. The most expensive thing to a company is turnover: all their training, knowledge, and growth for that person goes right out the door every time someone leaves. Companies that fall into this bucket also ultimately show that they care about their employees, as this automatically means they have some sort of vacation plan, some sort of 401k match, and possibly some workplace flexibility. If you are in this bucket, a raise should be well within your reach without significant difficulties, as it would be standard practice for the market at hand. Again, we are going to use the market and your work ethic to bolster your position—all with the aim of negotiating for more money in your pocket!

If you have a score over 7:
Congratulations! You have landed a company that cares about its employees and is willing to pay for them. However, this does make it more difficult to negotiate for a large raise— although it's still not impossible, especially with my proven system! You do have an advantage in the fact that you are already paid well, which means they would rather pay you more than lose you, in most cases.

In all of these situations, we are focusing on your merit, plus the market conditions, in order to build a funnel that only leads to you getting a raise (or you finding a new job that will pay you what you're worth!). Now that we have established your current place and current market value, let's review where you want to be.

What is your ideal salary for your current position?

_____

_____

_____

What is your ideal benefits package?

_____

_____

_____

What is your non-negotiable for your raise? For example, you definitely want to work from home, even if you don't get a payraise, or you want 5% more regardless if anything else changes.

_____

_____

_____

Now we know where you currently are and where you want to be, let's start building your ladder to success.

Before you can negotiate for a raise, you have to set yourself up to make a raise the only option (or a promotion, but we will get to that later): essentially, you are closing all the doors that would give the employer a way out of giving you a raise.

The typical excuses include:
- We only give raises a certain time of year;
- You were not rated "Exceeding"/ "Above and Beyond"/ "10/10" at your performance review;
- You take too much time off;

- You're not a team player;
- You are capped out within your pay grade;
- We don't have the money to give you a raise.

Out of these scenarios, you should have a preparation and response to them. As a pre-step, let's review the excuses to see if they apply to you.

1. **We only give raises at a certain time during the year.** Is this true for your company? Are you a part of a standard performance review schedule, where once a year, your performance and achievements are reviewed? If so, then we are planning for that time during the year. Don't set yourself up for failure by expecting the impossible to happen and for you to get a raise within the next month if your company only gives raises in six.

2. **You were not rated "Exceeding", etc. at your last performance review.** Okay, this is more of a statement of fact than anything else. Do you know what the expectations are for "Exceeding"? Are they clearly outlined and written down? If your expectations are not clearly listed, that will be an action item for you. Hold onto that for now.

3. **You take too much time off.** Are you taking off all of your allotted vacation? Are you giving correct notice? As long as you are giving notice, this should *never* stop you from receiving a raise or promotion. This is a HR complaint, and you should be looking for employment

elsewhere if told this. You earn vacation time to *use* it, not to let it look shiny and capped out on your paycheck.

4. **You're not a team player.** This one is a slippery slope—and if you are a people manager, this is especially dangerous. Highlight this as a focus point for improvement. If you are not a people manager, this is still dangerous: was this reflected in your last performance review? Are there courses available at your workplace that can help you to improve upon this? Did your boss give you action items for this? Make sure you keep this one at the forefront of your mind as we build your raise plan below.

5. **You're capped out within your pay range.** Super-duper. So you mean I'm getting a promotion? This is what this statement is saying. There are non-monetary ways to be incented if you want to go down this path (especially if you like the position)—or, your best option is typically to plan a path to promotion. Don't stay at a job where you can't make any more, yet you are still required to do more work.

6. **We can't give you any more money because we don't have it.** Now, at small companies, this may be true, but at any decent-sized corporation, this is just a copout. Don't back down: set yourself up for a raise. If they won't give it to you, it's time to move on.

With all of these statements, the raise plan will get you set up for success—but, as with any plan, there can and will be obstacles. Stay the course, and always remember that there are other employers! Don't stay at a company that isn't interested in your development and wellbeing; you can always find something better.

However, let's hope that is not needed! Now that you are aware of the most plausible objections, let's walk through the steps required in order to get a raise.

First things first, set your goal of how much you'd like to receive and what your non-negotiables are. Keep those at front and center at all times so you always have your eye on the prize. Remember those pay rankings before (1-10 that you gave the company) and bring that number back out.

Step 1: Review (Or Create) Your Expectations

Now, I'm not talking about your payraise-related expectations here; I'm talking about your expectations for your *position*. Before you can negotiate that you are awesome and deserve a raise, you need to set clear expectations for your role and your advancement. Start with your company goals; then, look at the large projects that you are working on. Find a commonality between your projects and the company goals, tie them together, and set these aside. If you're struggling to come up with projects or goals, start by writing a list of everything you do in a day (and everything that is on your backlog) and reorganize them by priority, and see what the biggest buckets within your list are. For instance, 30% of the list is data analysis, 20% is legal review, etc. Do these align with your position? And do they align with any company goals (e.g., increased profitability; streamlining processes)? Draw a clear connection when you can. Prioritize your final list and weight it. Now, you're ready for the next step.

Step 2: Create an Action Plan with Your Boss

Take the list you created and create a meeting for your boss, titled *Expectation and Performance Review*. This shows you want to go beyond your expectations, and that you're tying it to your performance. This may sound silly, but it's a very important distinction: *you're* setting up this conversation because you want it to be clear that the list you are providing is for your advancement. You want to be successful, and you need your boss to be on-board and to sign on in order to do so. If you can get things in line here, you're well on your way to success for getting a promotion.

Caution: If your work score was less than 4, your boss may not be interested in having this conversation with you—and this is typically a good indication that it is time to move companies. Any company that values its employees would want you to have a frank discussion about your goals and expectations because that leads to success. Success for you is success for them; success for all is success for the company.

Step 3: Align Your Expectations to Company/Corporate Metrics with Your Boss's Boss

If you have this option and the company is somewhat horizontal enough, take the opportunity to discuss your initiatives with your boss's boss: here, you can discuss what you and your boss went over, but also the bigger questions, such as:

1. How does my role fit in with the corporate objectives?
2. How can my expectations align more closely to helping the company (growth; increased revenue, etc.)?
3. Where do you see the team as a whole going in the next two/three years? (This gives outside perspective and shows that you are in this for the long haul.)
4. Where would you like to see my role strategically in the next year? If you could pick the biggest objective for me for the year, what would it be? (This is *huge*: it shows you value their opinion, that you're confirming your expectations, and that you want to succeed in their eyes. Talk about raise potential!)

This is a great step, if you can manage it, so I highly recommend you take the opportunity to do so. This also helps in the case of your manager ever switching/leaving/getting fired, as well as of your manager not holding up their end of the bargain. This gives you more skin in the game and shows leadership qualities.

If your work score is 7 or higher, this step is crucial: you are already well-paid and at a company that values its employees; hence, connecting your individual success to company success is imperative to be able to convey higher value.

Step 4: Outperform Your Metrics

This is truly where push comes to shove. You've got your expectations; your manager is on-board; your leadership team agrees and is aware. Time to shine! Dedicate yourself to your goals and doing whatever it takes to make them happen. Regardless of your work score, you must succeed at this step; without this, you don't even have a leg to stand on! Even if the target is moving throughout the year, make sure you record your wins, awards, and weekly accomplishments toward the goals being worked towards at that time. Set up a system to "report" to yourself weekly, as this makes it easier to show all of your accomplishments toward whatever the current goal was at the time at the end of the year.

Step 5: Set Up Progress Meetings

This should occur during Step 2—and, if this is the case, make sure you set up progress meetings with your manager with the specific intention of discussing your goals and progress. Do not let this meeting turn into a working session for what is currently going on! I recommend still having your 1:1, weekly meetings, etc. with your boss and scheduling this either during a lunch hour, or when you have an opportunity to step away from your day-to-day. You also want this to occur at least every 90 days, if not more frequently, and the objective is to review where you are, where you're going, and your current assessment. This should also include their review of your growth potential and role expansion. Ask for honest feedback, and, if everything is positive, ask for one thing that you can improve on before your next meeting—even if you seem perfect in their eyes! Many people (including bosses) are scared to give honest feedback due to retaliation in their own performance review—or, worse, a mutiny on their team! However, if you specifically ask for it, you can normally at least solicit something small. This may hurt your ego, but if you show you can take feedback and actually work on whatever the issue may be, you show your maturity, as well as your leadership qualities. There is nothing more attractive to an employer than someone who is self-aware and trying to improve for the sake of the company.

If your work score is between 4 and 7, this step is very crucial, as companies in this group need to be reminded of the great work that you're doing, whilst simultaneously being kept accountable to what you initially set out for. They need to be reminded that your eye is on the prize, as this will give your manager a sense of urgency and focus regarding your position. Fair warning: some bosses (especially micro middle management) may *hate* these meetings, and this is why Step 3 was so important. If your boss continually blows this meeting off or doesn't give you clear feedback or guidance, go to the next level; you need to have this for success. You can't reach your goals if you don't have them!

Step 6: Get Ready For The Raise Negotiation!

You've made it past your check-ins; you're checking all the boxes; and people are noticing your improved performance and your job clarity. They *see you*—so now is the time to ask for exactly what you want. You have your expectations, how you've performed against them, and how you've outperformed them; you've already discussed your expectations and the typical bonus/reward to exceeding your expectations... So it's time to claim your reward! Don't forget that this is still a negotiation; the boss may not have the power to give you everything you want or ask for, but you want to make sure you've closed any doors for opportunities to escape. You want to get them to a point where they'll gladly give you what you want because they don't want to lose you—and they know that if they don't, you'll leave. They are in the fatal funnel, so it's time to go in for the kill and to get exactly what you want. You're ready for Section 2.

If you have a score less than 4, this is your opportunity for a *big* raise: you've met everything; you're crushing your goals; and your management is aware. However, if the company is rated poorly, there is a chance even *before* you commence negotiation that they will back out of everything. If this is the case, time to find a new company!

If you are between 4 and 7, this may be the opportunity for a raise or a promotion. Such clarity and strength around your goals typically get noticed by upper management, and may have you on the fast track for promotion.

If you are over a 7, this is where you need to prove your extraordinary worth: write down all the goals at hand and brag about your overachieving of them. You've been successful this year, and need to prove that you have been so successful that you deserve even more, and that you are indispensable.

Keep these ideas in mind as we enter into negotiation in Section 2.

CHAPTER 4:
PATH TO PROMOTION

S O, YOU'VE DECIDED THAT a raise isn't enough, or a promotion is what you are truly seeking. Sometimes, this comes out of the woodwork from Raising the Bar, and they offer the promotion to you—but it can also be your goal, too. Before negotiating for a promotion or accepting one that is offered to you, however, you need to assess what the promotion means to you in terms of:

- Job responsibilities;
- Hours;
- Pay change;
- Future growth;
- Leadership/team skills;
- Career path.

All of these are important for your baseline, since a promotion should always bring more money! As the saying "with more power comes more responsibility" goes, if you're being promoted, you're going to have more responsibility—and if you have more responsibility, you should be paid more. Many companies may offer a promotion in lieu of a payraise, which should send up red flags for you: a promotion is not an option in lieu of a raise; only in addition to. Therefore, if your goal is a promotion, your goal is also a raise—which is why we started there first.

Now, onto promotion specifics: you've gone through the steps for a raise and set yourself up for expectations, review cadence, etc. We will follow a very similar process for a promotion before adding the raise expectations on during the negotiation process. Let's take you back to your expectations.

You listed what your ideal salary and ideal benefits package were, so let's expand on this now.

If you were promoted, what would your ideal position look like?

_____

_____

_____

_____

_____

_____

Does the promotion include you as an individual contributor, or a team leader?

_____

_____

_____

_____

_____

_____

What new responsibilities would you want in your new position?

_____

_____

_____

_____

_____

Are you willing to relocate, if necessary?

_____

_____

_____

What are your non-negotiables in a promotion (i.e., more time off; growing the team size; better office)?

_____

_____

_____

Does the promotion you are seeking exist within the current structure of the company you work for? (If the answer to this is no, you may have to look elsewhere to achieve your goals!)

_____

_____

_____

Are there any open positions in the career path you are looking at in your current company?

_____

_____

_____

Now, we have your baseline for what you expect out of a promotion, as well as the salary and benefits requirements. We have also established if there are current promotions available at your current company, or if you may have to look elsewhere. This will be important in the following steps.

The last piece we have established are your non-negotiables, and this will be extremely important when we get to the negotiation stage. When we look at a promotion or overall career progression, your non-negotiables are your boundaries, and you must stay within them at all costs. If you sway too far one way or the other, you will almost always regret it. Take the following example to illustrate this:

Say you are offered an incredible promotion with more money, but it requires you to relocate across the country without your family (at least short-term). You're commuting on the weekends back home, and you say yes to such an arrangement because the money is amazing—but realize shortly after moving that you feel lonely, isolated, and unfulfilled. One of your non-negotiables was a work-life balance, and, as a result of being blinded by the money, you're actually moving farther away from your goals. You're becoming unfulfilled and unhappy because you didn't stay true to your core principles to start with.

Now, this isn't to say that such a decision wouldn't have great learnings, or lead to amazing opportunities; however, even still, if your non-negotiable was time with your family, especially as they get older, you will probably regret this. If we bring attention to this in the beginning, you can hopefully avoid this situation and lead to building your ideal corporate experience and life! We now have your expectations and ideals, and can start the path to promotion.

Step 1: Moving Up the Ladder

One of the most important steps when earning a promotion is being seen as an asset by management, whether that be your direct manager, a manager within a similar team, or any multi-tiered managers common within large corporations in your sector (similar to your regional manager, division manager, vice president, etc.). When you decide that a promotion is the next step in your journey, pick an advocate: is there someone above you on the ladder who likes you; someone who's noticed your growth/success over the time you've been in your role? If so, set up a meeting with this person as a career discussion and align your goals with theirs. Let's say this person is a more senior colleague: they are not your direct manager, but are on a similar team, with a role similar to your manager. You may set up a discussion with an email like the following:

Hello, [XYZ],

I hope all is well. Thank you for the recent feedback on [XYZ] Project. I greatly appreciate the guidance and mentorship you've been able to give me. I wanted to set up some time to discuss this further, if possible. Please let me know when you would be available for a quick chat or coffee.

Thanks,

[Your Name]

You want to keep this short and simple; this is more about the conversation and dialogue than the email. This is just opening the door. Some people may have a comfortable enough relationship to ask the person directly, but formalizing the purpose of a meeting in an email can make things easier for you to progress; you don't want this to be an "all about you" conversation, but you also want there to be some structure.

Once the meeting is set, I recommend opening with your standard conversation (i.e. however you would interact with the person normally). Once you get past this cordial initial conversation, however, I'd be frank with the person: it's always good to make your intentions known in this space, as you want this person as your ally! For instance:

Hey, [XYZ],

Thanks again for all your suggestions and guidance on this project. It really helped me grow and learn [XYZ] skills. I'm looking to expand my role and further extend my skills in [XYZ], which I know you're an expert in. I'd love to learn from the best, so it is with that in mind that I ask: How did you expand your skills? Would you be able to share any courses/materials you learned from? I'd also love to be able to have you as a mentor for this, if you wouldn't mind. Nothing formalized, but once or twice a quarter, we could sit together and go over some hot topics. I know you're interested in having a larger team, and I would love to be a tester for any of your leadership techniques (ha-ha). A light, candid conversation!

Would you be interested in that?

If you know the person pretty well, they will most likely be really open to helping. This also helps if you know the other person is in management and is trying to level up, as you are essentially giving them the opportunity to "coach" you—one of the pillars for leadership. On the flipside, however, you're also learning a new skill and developing a relationship, and, as they move up, you may also. If your name comes up for a promotion, you have an inside seat for a vote your way.

Building relationships is one of the most important skills for promotions, as talent alone is not enough to be promoted in most companies anymore; you have to have buy-in—which brings us to Step #2.

Step 2: Leadership Buy-In

This may come from your manager or manager's manager— someone in your direct line. As tough as it may be (especially with corporate dynamics), manager buy-in is extremely important at larger companies. In addition to your recruited friend mentioned in Step #1, you will need a leadership mentor to give you the nod when you go for a promotion. I like to start this conversation in a similar way as that detailed in Step #1, but more focused, since your boss is your golden ticket: they can make or break you. If you get the boss's buy-in, it makes an in-company promotion a much smoother process. You want to set up the introduction in a way that makes it a positive, engaging experience for them (and a promotion for you!). Start by asking them for some time to discuss your progress this year and career-planning, and, if you've been doing your 90-day (as a minimum!) check-ins, your boss should have an idea of how things are going—and you should, too! Discuss your progress and then transition the conversation with something like this:

I know that I have been doing well and wanted to talk about my career path over the next year. I'd like to consider [XYZ] position, and wanted to see if you could help me to enhance my skills so that I would be a great candidate for an open position, if it were to come up. I really appreciate your guidance and help, as well as your leadership in helping me to achieve whilst I exceed expectations for the team.

Saying this establishes a few things:

1. **You want their help and value their leadership.** Super important so they don't think you're gunning for their position or excluding them from the process! This also adds to their leadership skills, as when you get promoted, *they* look good: they trained you, even if only partially!
2. **You're establishing your goals.** Firm and clear.
3. **You're asking for help, and using the improvements you make on yourself in the meantime.** Your boss may only be giving honest feedback to prepare you for your next position, but that will also help their team in the meantime.

Using this conversation starter should help to ease your boss into helping you to help yourself (and help them in the process!).

Once everyone is on the same team, it's time to work on the needed skills for the promotion. If you had all the skills already, you would have been promoted already—so if that isn't the case, it is time to sharpen some of the extra skills that are necessary for advancement! From the same folks you spoke to in Step #1 and Step #2, see where you may be lacking. Be honest with these people, and ask for candid feedback; it's the only way you'll grow! Don't let your emotions get involved; it will stop your peers from giving you honest feedback. Remember, your focus is to get a promotion—and you have to gain some tough skin in the process in order to do so!

This process will not be as quick as a raise in many situations; you're gaining skills and using your networking skills within the company to enlarge your circle. You also need to wait for an appropriate position to be opened up or created for you before this occurs. Build your skills and build your patience; your time will come.

The final step of the path to promotion or negotiating a raise, new position, or career change is here: we are ready for negotiating.

The time has come.

SECTION 2:

THE NEGOTIATION

CHAPTER 1:
PREPARING FOR
AN INTERVIEW

WHETHER YOU ARE APPLYING FOR a new position at a new company or within your current company, it is important to prepare yourself for the interview process.

Here is where my incredible additional material comes in particularly useful; this is essential for the rest of this section's potential to be maximized—and that is so important because this is what is ultimately going to get you a raise. Grab yours at https://beautyandaboss.clickfunnels.com/joinus.

The key to nailing the negotiation is staying calm, and one of the best ways to do that is to come prepared. Before you start your interviews, you should always have a few things in your "Go Bag", your virtual/in-person briefcase that should be refreshed and brought to each and every interview you attend. Some of these items will stay the same for the entirety of your interviewing process, but many will change with each interview—particularly if you are interviewing for a variety of positions (e.g., business analyst, sales operations specialist, and accounting administration assistant). In this situation, you may have skills that match all of these titles, but may need to revise your answers to meet the exact description for that position.

Your 8 to Great "Go Bag" items include:
- Updated copies of your resume (at least five);
- A 60-second *Get to Know Me* introduction;
- Prepped answers for the most common interview questions;
- Explanations for any resume oddities;
- Biographies of the people who are interviewing you, if possible;
- Information about the company;
- General information about the position;
- Industry hot topics at a high level.

Now, let's dig a little deeper.

Updated Copies of Your Resume

This is important for many reasons, but mainly, you want folks to be able to contact you and know about you quickly and efficiently. Many people will get an email before your interview with your resume, but most don't take a look at them; hence, your chance to captivate is when they are right in front of you. Even if they have a copy already, it looks extremely professional to be able to provide a copy for everyone there. 80% of the interview is non-verbal, and this is one of the first steps to show your professionalism and organization. Make sure you have at least five copies, or more if they have mentioned you will be doing group interviews. Make sure your name, address, and phone are up-to-date on all the copies, and that the content is current and tweaked with the keywords listed in each job description. This will help when applying whilst you are being highlighted by the HR systems.

60-Second *Get to Know Me* Introduction

I cannot stress enough how important this introduction is in the interview process; this often happens before you even meet with the hiring manager, and is typically over the phone with a HR Manager or recruiter. However, it also comes in handy when you are being interviewed with multiple team members, as well as when you eventually get the hiring manager. The 60-second introduction should go over a host of things, but in the form of a short, condensed description; it's like a "get-to-know-me" question, but is opening your history with items that are not on your resume that may pique the interest of your interviewer. When constructing this, think of an elevator speech for a business, or something that you really like: what are the most important items to mention if you only have enough time until the elevator gets from the top floor to the bottom floor?

You want to mention items such as:

1. Quick schooling history (i.e., your degree/relevant coursework);
2. Your current role and the skills you've developed that are related to the role you're applying for;
3. Anything missing from your resume that is interesting and directly related to your career (e.g., I have a gap of six months on my resume when I traveled the world to expand my understanding of economic diversity);
4. The reason why you applied for the job, or what sparked your interest in the position (and of course, tie it back to your background). How did you get to this point where you are now looking to leave your old position and explore something new? Keep the language here positive.

I recommend sticking with just a few items in your introduction; it shouldn't be overly long, or a repeat of your resume. The recruiter (or, indeed, any of your interviewers) is just trying to get a real-world sense of who you are *outside* of your resume.

Real. Relevant. Responsible.

This brings us to the next section of preparation.

Prepared Answers to Common Interview Questions

Keep those three words in mind at all time. You want any answer you give to be:

1. **Real**. It actually happened, and you didn't make it up. Everyone can research everything nowadays, so there's no use in lying!

2. **Relevant.** Keep the interview on-track. Small anecdotes are nice and show that you are a human person who has feelings and not just a name on a screen, but don't go off on a tangent that requires a lot of background and doesn't demonstrate your skills in application to the position! This may not only be confusing for your interviewer, but also opens up more opportunity for you to say something offensive or unprofessional without realizing it. Stick to the story about how you are the best corporate citizen there is and how you want to share your gifts with this wonderful new company.

3. **Responsible.** You never know who is interviewing you and what their moral objections and beliefs are, so stick to stories and answers that are straight and narrow. This doesn't mean you can't talk about your time studying abroad in Europe; just leave out the part where you had a blast while learning how to drink like a fish! Talk about the culture, the adaptation required to a new location at a young age with a new language, and the resulting personal growth. Don't talk about the drinking. (Or that threesome you had one time with your softball friends.)

(I'm not joking here: these two examples have actually happened to me in real-life interviews. It doesn't matter what my personal beliefs are on the subjects: this is super inappropriate for interview discussion. Stick to work topics. If you are unsure whether something is appropriate, leave it out, and ask yourself, "Would my grandmother be proud to hear me say this on a stage in front of 1,000 other grandmothers?" If the answer isn't 100% yes, don't bring it up. Refer back to #1. Try again.)

As a general rule of thumb: Leave out politics, religion, and drunken shenanigans. Better to keep that until *after* you've gotten a job—or just out of the workplace forever!

Okay, so back to the meat and potatoes of the situation: in all of the questions below, think about the list of the trio above when answering. You may be asking yourself, "Why do I need to prep these? I always say the same thing.", or, "They never ask the same questions, this is pointless." Well, let me stop you there: over 70% of the interviews I have been a part of (because I keep track of all the questions, you know; #MathNerd over here) have some variation of the same questions listed below. Yes, the phrasing might be slightly different, but it's the same question, at its core. Secondly, how sure are you that you answer the same every time? Have you ever played a game of telephone? By the time the phrase gets to the end, the message is totally different. I would bet that at least half of the time, your answer is not the same. Interview stress is a real thing, and so by preparing these answers and having them in front of you, you have not only taken away some of the brain processing required for the current situation, but you've also kept yourself on-track and lowered your stress response. This keeps your brain clear from brain fog and allows you to focus on the task at hand. To sum it all up, this is great practice, and helps keep your message to come across clearly and concisely. Clear message = more professional appearance = more $$$.

Remember: **Real. Relevant. Responsible.**

Now, to the questions: I've given you lots of space, so write or type your answers in the space below. I recommend doing a first round on a piece of scrap paper, or on your computer, so that you can read it back and edit it as needed. If you've never done this before, the first version you answer is normally clunky, and this is the exact reason we are doing this. Clean; professional; polished; perfection.

Can you review your resume for me (i.e., go over your background; give me an introduction of yourself; tell me more about you; give me a job history)?

_____

_____

_____

_____

_____

_____

Now, before we move on, reread your answer. Does it check all three boxes?

Real ☐
Relevant ☐
Responsible ☐

Tell me more about your current role (i.e., how does your current role relate to this role?). Give specifics: use system names, the number of employees you manage, etc.

_____

_____

_____

_____

_____

_____

Does it check all three boxes?

Real ☐
Relevant ☐
Responsible ☐

What do you know about the position? Why would you be a good fit for the position?

_____

_____

_____

_____

_____

_____

Does it check all three boxes?

Real ☐
Relevant ☐
Responsible ☐

Tell me about a time when you had to persuade someone to do something that they didn't like (e.g., when you had to solve a disagreement and the outcome; how you handled a troubling situation/coworker/team member).

_____

_____

_____

_____

_____

Does it check all three boxes?

Real ☐
Relevant ☐
Responsible ☐

How do you deal with confrontation? Are you an introvert or extrovert? How do you manage a team?

_____

_____

_____

_____

_____

_____

Does it check all three boxes?

Real. ☐
Relevant. ☐
Responsible. ☐

Where do you see yourself in five years? 10 years? (Think about your career goal; whether you like to stay with one company; and your career path).

_____

_____

_____

_____

_____

_____

Does it check all three boxes?

Real   ☐
Relevant   ☐
Responsible   ☐

What is your ideal job/career? (What do you want to do in 10 years? Is this a stepping stone, or an end goal?)

_____

_____

_____

_____

_____

_____

Does it check all three boxes?

Real ☐
Relevant ☐
Responsible ☐

Tell me of a time when you messed up. How did you handle the situation?

_____

_____

_____

_____

_____

Does it check all three boxes?

Real ☐
Relevant ☐
Responsible ☐

What is your greatest accomplishment (i.e., the best thing you've ever done; the thing you are most proud of; your crowning achievement)?

_____

_____

Does it check all three boxes?

Real. ☐
Relevant. ☐
Responsible. ☐

And lastly, what salary do you expect for this position (i.e., what is your earning potential; how much did you make at your last position, etc.)?

I'm going to answer this one for you. This is an answer HR folks hate, but then again, they shouldn't really be asking this question, anyway.

Your response should be as follows:

My previous roles and responsibilities were not the same, so I'd rather not discuss my previous salary and would like to focus on the opportunity in front of me instead. What is the salary range for this position? Is there any negotiation on this range?

And then *refuse to talk about it further.*

In all likelihood, they are going to push back again and keep asking. **Do not give in**. This is *crucial* for the negotiation later on.

Only respond to that question if the salary range is far below what you are expecting, so that you can conclude the interview process; you are, after all, not interested in something that is half of what your base income needs are, etc. Otherwise, shut up and let the HR person answer. You can say the range is acceptable if they ask, but don't give any specifics.

You've now made it through the top 10 interview questions that cover the board. There is, however, one that I have left out on purpose, as it is big enough—in detail and in importance—to merit its own section.

Explanations for Any Resume Off-Time/Oddities

So, the big question that has been left out: "How do you explain the year without work?", or, "I see there is some time missing here; what happened?" Many people think this is an automatic buzzkill to the interview, but in many cases, it's not: if you've made it to getting an interview, then you've already made it past half the battle. One thing I highly recommend is going back and filling in gaps in your resume way before this step. If you have a large gap due to childbirth, pursuing an entrepreneurial venture, or simply went traveling, fill it in! Gaps in employment can send up flags in HR systems, and sometimes can even disqualify you.

First, fill in the information with the skills that you were working on; show the skills and developments you made while you were pursuing untraditional employment.

For instance, if you travelled around the world for a year "wanderlusting" and you are a corporate accountant, you may put on your resume:

Economic Assessment Explorer
- *Traveled year-round exploring the economic impacts of XYZ in ABC Regions.*
- *Implemented cost-saving measuring and extreme budgeting to increase business longevity.*
- *Learned cultural norms of 10 cultures throughout SE Asia, including monetary policies and the effects of tourism on small island life.*

Now, I know this sounds like a stretch, but the interviewer will *definitely* bring it up—and, believe it or not, that is exactly what you want: a chance to explain. If you leave the gap blank, no one knows what you did, and, to put it bluntly, it sounds like you sat around and gained nothing. If, however, you frame this in a positive way, you can show the "life skills" that you learned over that time, as well as how you added value to your position as an accountant: after all, you had to have known how to budget properly if you were living purely off savings for a year. This also shows that you are resourceful, cultured, and ready to take on any new challenges that come your way; after all, you lived out of a backpack for a year! What *can't* you handle?

If you look at the description I wrote up, you'll notice a few things: first, that there is no mention of negativity (everything is framed as a learning); second, that I cleverly listed items that would just be a normal everyday task (i.e., budgeting) to make it sound more relevant to the position (tying back to the three rules in the previous section, in turn allowing you to play the system to your advantage); and third, I came up with a unique name that will spark interest in a conversation. You want to talk about your journey, especially if it is your most recent "job history". It will be important that you can demonstrate professionalism whilst explaining the skills you learned abroad while volunteering or being a homemaker—and a resume listing like this will give you that exact opportunity.

So, now that you have the opportunity, don't waste it: make sure you have a good explanation of *why* you did what you did, and *why* you are returning to normal life. Running out of money is not a good answer; saying that you wanted more traditional stability, on the other hand, is. You have to phrase your answers so that HR folks and hiring managers see you as a desirable candidate. It is also crucial to mention the tools you continued to use in your interview, like Excel or PowerPoint: if you were refreshing your skills along the way, it will be super-easy for you to jump back in.

Pro Tip: If you weren't refreshing your skills, jump in now. Take an Excel course with a certificate or a small cheap program related to your field so that you can show your relevancy to the current market. This may seem like a small step, but it's a great way to show your dedication.

So, you have explained what you did and why you did it, and now you've explained why you're returning. You should also make sure to explain why your most recent experience will add to the workplace/position you are applying for, instead of hindering it; for instance, homemakers are very compassionate, task-oriented, and organized, so highlight those items! Meanwhile, work travelers may be frugal, creative, and solution-oriented—perfect for *agile* environments (note my use of buzzwords!).

All in all, however, ensure you are posing your recent traditional workplace hiatus as a positive, not a negative. Don't try to hide it or cover it up; own it and explain it. The workplace needs diversity, and this is just one way in which you can show how diverse you are!

The next few items are things you need to look for prior to the interview. Unlike the questions above, these may change with each interview, so be prepared to research each time you have a new interview coming up. You don't have to be a private investigator, but you should still dedicate some time into researching, writing down some key bullet points in the process. You can sprinkle them in your answers to connect with your manager/interviewer and make your other answers more relevant.

Biographies of the People Who Are Interviewing You, If Possible

Normally, when you are scheduled for an interview, the HR Manager will give you the name and job title of the person(s) that you will be speaking with. Hence, before it's time to have your interview, take to LinkedIn or Google and give a quick search to the name and the company. It is more than likely that you will find the person you are looking for (or at least narrow it down to just one or two folks), and, from there, you can familiarize yourself with the inner workings of your interviewer, as well as find some commonalities between the two of you. You may also want to look at where they went to school, as well as their recent positions. Have they been at the company for a long time? Is this a new transition for them? Getting insight into these things may not only help with interview questions, but it may also serve the secondary purpose of helping you to decide if this is a company you want to work with.

Remember, throughout this whole process of being interviewed, you are also consciously interviewing the other side to make sure the company is a good fit. For example, if you come to learn that they have only been there for three months, you can then ask yourself whether you're comfortable with a boss or a new team. This, then, may prompt a great interview question for you, such as, "What is the plan for the team you are joining over the next year?", or, "How has your experience been at the company?" You're not going to get the nitty-gritty, but you would be surprised at how much you'll find out by asking a question like that. If there are hints of negativity already, this might not be the best opportunity for you in the end.

Pro Tip: I'm not saying to sabotage the interview or ask a crazy off-the-wall question from your LinkedIn investigation; what I am saying is to keep an open mind, but remember why you are looking for the new position in the first place. Scrutinize your interviewer so you don't waste your time.

To close it all off, find out a bit about your interviewers so that you can relate to them, understand a glimpse into their past, and possibly get a few interview questions for when they inevitably ask, "So, do you have any questions for me?"

Information about the Company

This process follows closely in line with the LinkedIn or Google (or whatever search engine you prefer) research, but goes a step further: as mentioned in the last section, you want to make sure the company you are interviewing with...

1. **Is a legit company.** This is a real concern in the current environment. Unless it's a big corporation that you're dealing with, you may not have heard of the people reaching out to you. Now, this doesn't mean that they aren't a real business, or they don't have what you want, but it still can't hurt to try and verify some of the information. Make sure you do some research to try and protect yourself.

On this note... Typically, if a company reaches out to you and tells you to pay something upfront, that's a scam. Just saying. Do your research before making a decision.

2. **Meets your core values.** Has the company switched names 100 times? Do they lay off thousands every year at Christmas? If so, maybe this isn't a place that aligns with your values and goals.

3. **Matches your career goals.** Startups may be great for some folks (lower pay but stock value; more company mobility, etc.), whereas those with children or those searching for stable, long-term growth may only want large, stable companies. Make sure you understand what you're dealing with!

While you're looking at these sites, you can also take a look at company rating sites, like Glassdoor. These will not be perfect—anyone can post reviews, so even the disgruntled worker who constantly showed up late and got fired can leave a review—, but it should still give a general overview of the company you're walking into.

On these sites, be sure to see how many reviews are listed: if there are less than 20, I wouldn't give it much weight. Also, be sure to check the locations. Notably, one of the nice things about Glassdoor (as of 2020, that is!) is that you can see salary bands, as well as insights into benefits packages. They might even have common interview questions listed there.

I recently went through this exercise with a client and she found the exact position she was applying for on Glassdoor. The person had listed the salary they were offered, and even all the interview questions she would be asked. Now, was it 100% true? No; but 85% of her interview questions (including two tricky technical questions) were posted. What a leg-up she had, simply because she prepared ahead of time! This was the value that arose as a result of taking an hour and doing some research. We also had a very solid idea of the starting salary they were going to offer her—and, by following the strategies I'll discuss later in this book, she didn't cut herself off at the knees by low-balling her own pay! A little bit of research goes a long way. She ended up getting an offer $10,000 higher than she was expecting.

Glassdoor, LinkedIn, Google, and other similar sites are a great way to gain invaluable insight into the company at hand. Whilst investigating, you also want to look for warning signs; this may include lots of people commenting that a work-life balance doesn't exist, or that upper-level management doesn't care about its workers. In the corporate world, this is especially important when considering the fact that you are making this career move for a reason. Don't stop the interview process, but when it gets down to offer time, keep these facts in mind to bolster your needs—or, alternatively, explore the other offers that may be coming your way. It would also be a good idea to look for things that match your needs (e.g., mention of unlimited vacation; a 6% 401K match). When you're on these sites, you'll get great insight into the company and its overall vibe; however, you should also be on the lookout for position-specific details, as we'll discuss in our next section.

General Information about the Position

Since you're in deep now on LinkedIn and Glassdoor, you might as well look into the exact position you've applied for. You may only find the actual job description, but on some occasions, you'll be able to pick up on little extras. Maybe you misread the job description and you see additional skills listed at the bottom of the long description.

Pro Tip: Read the job descriptions fully. So many folks throw quick questions into the end of the job description to see if people are reading them, and this can be one of the easiest ways to get selected for a job or an interview from a large application pool. This will be especially invaluable to you if you're struggling to get interviews.

You may be pleasantly surprised and run into a situation like I mentioned with one of my clients, where all the interview questions and pay ranges were listed. Regardless of whether this ends up being the case or not, it's better to know ahead of time, and may give you a firmer grasp on the interview questions to ask.

Industry Hot Topics at a High Level

Last, but certainly not least, industry topics. If you're staying in the same industry as your previous job, this may be easy, since such hot topics relate to your day-to-day; however, even if this is the case for you and is an area you're confident in, I still encourage you to take a look at hot industry topics on Google or LinkedIn, just to make sure you know what the current buzzwords are, what the most important current issues are, and what positions are in high demand. Meanwhile, if you're new to the industry, you should know all of this, in addition to the basics of the industry (e.g., the language; common slang; the used tools and systems; commonly held certifications). You don't have to be an expert, but being well-versed in your industry helps to show the interviewer that you did your research and are committed to the industry you'll be a part of. This is also crucially important if you are in an industry that is impacted by public policy (e.g., accounting; finance; healthcare), as big public policy decisions can weigh heavily on upper-level management, hiring, and payscale. If this is a tense time in your industry, such circumstances may impact your ability to negotiate. If, however, this is a stable time with lots of demand, you're in the perfect position to negotiate and gain an upper hand from the beginning.

Indeed, regardless of the current situation, you need to know the attitude of the corporation in the environment: by addressing this in the interview, you are showing awareness, professionalism, and good corporate citizenship, which many large corporations greatly value and are definitely willing to pay for.

Once you have all of these things, your go bag is ready! Now, the final piece to prepare for the interview: your outfit!

The Interview Day Outfit

This is one of the most overlooked aspects of any interview. It doesn't matter what anyone tells you: appearance matters. That's not to say that you have to be a beauty queen or prom king to land the job; rather, that you should always look professional, presentable, and personable.

Your outfit should consist of a few things on your interview day:

1. **A well-fitted suit.** If you can't afford a custom-tailored suit from a name brand place (e.g., Nordstrom; Macy's), go to a thrift shop and look for a nice suit that fits you decently and looks great—no frays and a nice color—, and then take it to a tailor to get it fitted. You can find suits for under $50 (sometimes for even cheaper or for free on Facebook Marketplace!). A decent tailor may, however, require $100 to fix the suit jacket, as long as nothing is too major, but I can assure you that the money is well worth it. Looking clean and professional is very important. I recommend sticking with black, gray, or navy as a suit color for any corporate job. I personally use my suit jacket as a statement piece (my famous red blazer is always a hit,

and something for folks to remember me by), but unless you have the personality for it, I wouldn't recommend a main staple in your closet to be an outlandish suit piece to start. You want to convey professionalism; clean lines; taste. Think about a lawyer or the President: what would they wear? Many folks will say this isn't necessary, or that they don't need a jacket, and I've never found that to be true: the fact of the matter is that it totally changes the way the interviewee looks at you. I also wouldn't recommend a dress for ladies; I would stick to the pantsuit. A dress that is too short can send the wrong signals, and you don't want to be giving them any reason to say no before you even have the opportunity to convince them to say yes! Discrimination does exist in the workplace, but you need to not give in to it—and wearing appropriate clothing is one way to do that. Remember, you are trying to negotiate for a higher paying job, or a new career, so don't sabotage yourself by trying to be unique with your outfit when you don't know the opinions or feelings of those you will be working for. You can't influence their decisions if you're starting at a disadvantage. Your outfit is your level-setting, and you're here to win. That's it.

2. **A button-down shirt.** I know companies are going casual, and that people can wear jeans and yoga pants to the office. I get it. But this is an interview, not the workplace, and, with that said, you should *not* be

casual in the interview. Wear a suit jacket, suit pants, and a button-down underneath. Be professional. Remember, you don't want to give them a reason to dislike you before they get a chance to know you!

3. **Moderate heels.** Wear shoes that you can walk in. Generally, 1-3 inches is the best heel height; anything higher than that can give off the wrong interview vibes. If you can't walk in heels, no heel is fine; however, a good heel does make you stand up straighter and exude confidence, which is crucial for sealing the deal. The caveat to all of this: if you can't walk properly in your shoes, *don't wear them*. It's much better to wear flats and have your personality shine through with confidence in your resume without falling on your face, instead of wearing heels and tripping down the steps!

4. **One statement piece**. This can be jewelry, a colorful button-down, a fun belt, or a bag. This controls the outlandishness that might ensue if you choose more than one. Remember, you don't know your interviewer's beliefs; they may be very conservative and find color to be offensive, or simply find your presence to be overwhelming when they first meet you. You don't want your outfit to overpower your personality; you're looking for enhancement! One statement piece looks classy; six pieces looks trashy. Being seen as artsy in this corporate environment is not normally a good thing. It's also more than likely that you are going to be interviewed by a man, and people tend to like people

who are like them. Thus, if you're a woman in a fancy dress with a huge hat, he is immediately going to be on guard: you don't look like him, so how could you be like him? He may also be distracted by your outfit, in turn leading to him remembering your clothes over your answers. I know this is highly vain, but it's the truth: it is a bias that most people are not even aware that they have.

Pro Tip: My statement piece is now my red blazer; however, when I started, it was a purple jeweled necklace. People always commented on it, and it was a great icebreaker. I had a great story to go with it, too: it was from my grandmother and was a family heirloom, tying me into the business's core beliefs that family is important. This made me seem very trustworthy, which was, of course, exactly what I wanted in an interview. I switched to the red jacket when I started going for more advanced positions, as it embodied power and confidence—something that was reflected in my conversations. Folks asked different questions when I switched to this piece. I was more confident and able to earn a seat at the table with the big boys, simply because of how I carried myself. Always think: what does my outfit say about me? Do you like what it says? If you don't, change it!

5. **A professional briefcase/bag that has your resume, pens, a notebook or paper to write on, sticky notes, your wallet, and your cell phone.** Everything

you need to be prepared for the interview, and *only* the things you need for the interview. Some hand sanitizer, a small bottle of water, and some lipstick also wouldn't go amiss; who doesn't need those?

Once you have all of your attire together, put everything on a few nights before the interview. Make sure everything is ironed and that everything fits. Make sure to get plenty of rest and get up with enough time to do you makeup and hair professionally. There should be no need to rush on interview day, whether you're driving or Skyping. Give everything extra time; that way, you give the interviewer no reason to disqualify you over something that is totally within your control.

Now you're ready to Nail the Interview.

CHAPTER 2:
NAILING THE INTERVIEW

NAILING THE INTERVIEW HAS multiple steps, as most interviews at this point are multi-tiered in the corporate world:

- HR/Talent Manager
- Hiring Manager
- Team Members or additional cross-functional partners
- Final interviews (read: the negotiation!).

Each of these interviews is like the "The Floor Is Lava" game you played when you were a kid: any misstep, and you lose your life. Each one is important, but for different reasons: the HR interviewer tends to be the gatekeeper, asking basic resume questions, salary expectations, etc. They will also be the one who determines if the hiring manager ever gets to see your resume, so they are extremely important—even though the substance of that interview tends to be mostly high-level. The team interviews, meanwhile, are the exact opposite: you may get hired even if they don't go well, but in many cases, these are folks you'll be working with day in, day out; hence, any good hiring manager will take their opinion seriously. These conversations tend to be detailed and filled with substance, and allow you to really show your skills (and a bit of your personality!). Regardless of what interview stage you're in, all interviews are really important.

Remember: in order to get the highest value from this section, you'll really want to throw yourself in with the additional training I've made available for you, to allow you to really grow: https://beautyandaboss.clickfunnels.com/joinus.

Always start with the basics: be early (whether it is in-person or online), always dress professionally, turn your camera on if it's online, and always be prepared and have your "briefcase" ready for each interview. Prep for each one like it's a new interview, so that you're always fresh.

Let's move into the objectives of each interview and how to score high marks in each:

HR/Talent Manager

This is the first step in the process of your new career! If you're applying to an internal job for a promotion/job change, you may or may not have to go through the HR step. The purpose of this call is to get a feel for the candidate, review their resume for any inaccuracies, and sometimes to outline salary or work expectations. Some HR calls go more into more depth with questions around certain skillsets that are particularly important to the hiring manager. Notably, most HR calls are also not in person; they are almost always over the phone.

The keys to unlocking the next hiring stage are as follows:

1. **Be on time.** Always be ready for the call, or call into the dial early.

2. **Be honest.** Speak about your experience and use your elevator speech to expand further than your resume.

3. **Ask intelligent questions about the company**. Ask the basics about the position, location, and team. You want to show genuine interest in the company and position, so ask questions than are more than, "What are the duties of the role?" Instead, ask, "What does the day-to-day look like?", or, "What do you most enjoy about the company?" Both of these show that you are most invested in hearing about the company and the position than just the basics you can read online.

4. **Don't answer the salary question.** They are going to ask about what your salary expectations are; do not give in! Push back and ask what the range is for the position, and then see if it meets your needs. This doesn't mean you're going to fall within that realm (you can always start higher!), but it makes sure you are not wasting your time pursuing something that is well below your skillset and desired pay.

Luckily, the first stage is normally pretty easy: if you were truthful on your resume and you can speak clearly about the experience you have, this should be a breeze. Always remember to be friendly and personable. Listen with attention, not to just respond, and always end this stage by asking when you will be hearing more or when you can check in. Also ask what the next steps are, and then see the next section about following up.

Hiring Manager

The second step in the process is typically the hiring manager. This person will/would be your direct boss, and typically has the most influence on the hiring decision. This also tends to be the toughest interview in terms of the content related to the position, but with a few tricks, you can make this stage a breeze for yourself.

When dealing with the hiring manager, be sure to speak clearly and directly and to stay calm. The questions from the hiring manager typically come from the standard question list that you prepared ahead of time (go you!), so you should already be ready for those. Ensure you speak slowly and clearly; this will show confidence in your answers, which should be easy, since you already pre-prepped them and rehearsed them! If they throw an odd question at you, be sure to take a second to think: you won't be expected to answer right away! Be sure to fully answer their question: many people start on a tangent and then don't actually answer the question that is being asked.

Here, let's practice:

Can you explain a time to me where you were in a tough situation and had to make the best of it? What did you do?

[Film yourself on your phone, and then write the answer.]

_____

_____

_____

_____

_____

Does your answer actually answer the question? When you say things out loud, you can ramble on without realizing that you're not answering the question; when you write it, however, the answer becomes clear, and you can easily identify whether you actually missed the point.

Take a look back at your video: did you pause at the beginning to think before you answered? Do you sound positive in your answer? This is the perfect opportunity to practice your premade answers: go through each one and practice saying them with your phone, and keep on saying them until you feel confident in your answers. After this, ask a friend or loved one—or, better yet, go live on social media with the hashtag #BeABeautyAndABoss and tag us at @beabeautyandaboss, and we will help coach you to make sure you sound as professional as you can for interview day.

If the hiring manager gives you an actually odd question (e.g., "If you had to pick a favorite animal, what would it be and why?"), make sure to tie your answer back in to endearing qualities for the position. For instance, it doesn't matter if you answer dolphin or sloth, as long as the reasons are, "Their cognitive thinking is outstanding", or, "Their problem-solving abilities are great, and I value that", or, "They take time to think about their problems and react logically." This is just one way for them to see your personality.

As you are going through the questions with your hiring manager, don't forget to connect with them, laugh, and be personable; there's no need to be stiff and tight! If you're having issues with this (or you receive some feedback stating that this is a problem), reach out to their team; it can be hard to see past your own nose sometimes! Remember, you looked them up *before* this process, and should have a few notes about how you can connect.

The last piece for inclusion in the hiring manager interview is preparation for their question, "What questions do you have for me?" I recommend having a few pre-planned questions focused on a few areas:

1. **Daily tasks and day in the life.** You want to make sure this is a career you'll enjoy and feel comfortable doing (especially if your current job is by no means terrible, as you want to ensure you are moving *up* in your career!).

2. **Expectations for the first 90 days of this position.** This shows you're focused and task-oriented, ready to hit the ground running.

3. **Team future.** Long-term vision is important from a leader, and also gives a sense of loyalty and connection, since you are already thinking "like a team player".

4. **Company culture.** My personal favorite question is,

"What is your favorite and least favorite thing about the company?" This not only demonstrates your awareness of company culture and its importance, but also shows that you are human and know that not everything is going to be all sunshine and rainbows: you're actively looking for the best fit, and counters any assumptions that you are desperate for this position—which sets you up well for the negotiation!

5. **The expected hire date.** In larger companies, the hiring timeframe can be anywhere between 1-5 months (and I've seen longer!), so having an expectation of the timeline and next steps are crucial. Again, this shows you're expecting to be moved forward, as they haven't given you any reason to think you wouldn't. This also shows your confidence, and can actually sway a hiring manager to push you along if they were on the fence previously.

Above all else, the hiring manager will be asking about your skills, and may ask your background, as well as how you think it ties into the keywords in the position (and, of course, you've already prepared for this!). This is also the perfect time to get a feel for what your boss will be like. Go in there with an open mind: you want to make sure your unconscious bias is not coming through in the interview, as most of these are on the phone or on Skype/an electronic platform to begin with. Stay positive and calm!

Pro Tip: Respond with the same emotion with which your future boss is responding. If they raise their voice and sound excited, return with the same emotion; if they turn sombre and calm, keep the same attitude. People unconsciously like people who are like them, as they will feel a sense of similarity and understanding between the two of you—especially if your interviewer is a woman. This is not biased toward women; it's simply a statement about behavior. Women tend to make hiring decisions with more emotion than men, so connection is extremely important to them at a subconscious level.

So, you've reached the end of the interview with your hiring manager. It hopefully went exactly as planned—but even if it didn't, still be sure to send that follow-up listed in the next chapter! Buttoning up a deal can push you over the fence into the next opportunity or interview. Also always be sure to ask when you will hear back, or when you should reach out—and be sure to follow up in a timely fashion if that duty is on you!

Team Members and Additional Partners, With a Focus on Group Interviews

You've made it! The hiring manager must have liked you enough to push you through to the team, so you're moving in the right direction. In some cases, you might not even have this, and it's done; onto the negotiation! Saying this, in most larger firms, there will be a few additional people you'll need to meet with in order to seal the deal. This is also the most common time for folks to start in-person interviews. Typically, you will come in for 2–4 hours and meet with the hiring manager again in person (just to confirm everything they thought they knew about you!), as well as additional team members—either on an individual basis or in small groups. Some companies and roles may also require a presentation at this point—something that is becoming more and more common. This is because team members want to see the skills you said you had in action, particularly when we're talking positions that will be required in order to present/speak in front of executives on a regular basis, or higher level analysts that need to represent their data to non-analysts.

First things first, make sure you have your outfit ready to go. You should feel calm, confident, and ready to rock and roll. Secondly, make sure your virtual Go Bag is matched with your in-person Go Bag; in other words, that you have updated resumes, a notepad, and everything you would need if you had to give a presentation (i.e., jump drive; computer; charger, etc.). Make sure that you arrive to the interview at least 15 minutes early: it's always better to have a few minutes in the car talking to yourself and getting pumped instead of being late. Try to avoid scheduling interviews in-person around rush hour traffic, as this increases the unpredictability of traffic and the chances something will go wrong during the commute.

So, you've made it to the interview, and the group interviews are about to commence. At this point, most recruiters will send you an agenda ahead of time so you know who you're meeting with, which also gives you a chance to go back to the job posting and review. Ensure that you know the keywords, industry, and lingo. With such knowledge, these may flow naturally with your future teammates, which helps to breed connection. Don't miss that opportunity: make sure you are fresh with the latest and greatest. Group interviewers may also ask more reaching questions (i.e., things that are not directly related to the position, but more so the industry). Hence, having a strong grasp on what the hot topics are will really help you here. Don't forget about the company's competition, too!

Pro Tip: Look the folks up on LinkedIn so that when they are walking in the room to greet you, you already have an idea of who's who. This also gives you a split second to mentally prepare for what kind of person you read about, as well as what tone and questions to expect.

When team interviews begin, similar questions to those asked in the manager interview often arise. You may get some off-the-wall ones, or you may have an awkward interviewer—especially if it is a true team interview and the person is not a manager and doesn't have any direct reports—, but just roll through the questions. Stay calm and collected; you've practiced, and you're ready. You may very well be interviewed by a peer, since they want to see how you will fit with the team. This is totally normal, and should be expected. Carry yourself the same way as you would with a manager: focus on true, authentic connection, and how your stories demonstrate your skills. Watch and listen closely; don't start speaking before the other person is done (an interviewer's nightmare!); and listen for information and connection, not to respond. Whilst doing the latter, match the person's body language, just as you matched the tone and volume of the manager on the phone. Remember: similarity is a good thing in most situations here. However, above all else, be yourself; if these are going to be your co-workers, you want to enjoy working with them! Just don't say anything offensive, and stay away from the Big Three: religion, politics, and sex.

Group interviews with team members can make things a little more interesting, as there are more variables and more people in one room. The same rules apply as in any other interview situation: stay calm and focused, and if you researched them beforehand, you should have an idea of their backgrounds. This may even give some hints as to the types of questions they may ask. Whenever you're asked a question, speak directly to the person who asked, and make sure you actually answer the question—just like when you met with the hiring manager. If the folks start to talk about something you are unfamiliar with, try asking an inquisitive question, or making some remark (e.g., "Wow, that must have been an interesting time!"). This is a way to bring yourself into the conversation and feel connected as a group. Match the group tone and emotions; speak passionately about anything related to the workplace or your core beliefs. After all, this is your chance to put the company culture to the test. If you really connect with one person, they can be your behind-closed-doors advocate when the decision is being made. On the contrary, one super negative opinion can kill the deal for you, so try to connect with everyone on some level.

If you're not an extrovert and have difficulty with connecting with people, I recommend reaching out for interviewing skill sessions; these are crucial when it comes to landing a great position, and can help you to build the self-confidence to nail a group interview. People can feel your presence, and they know group interviews can be uncomfortable—and that's exactly why they do them! They're testing to see if you'll fit in, as well as how you handle pressure. In a particularly hot job market where good positions are snatched up quickly, this is one way to narrow down your candidate pool: managers want teams that naturally work well together, if they can get them, so what better way to test this than through a group interview?

The icing on the cake of a group interview is a presentation: many corporations add a presentation on, as they want to see your skills in action, as well as to assess your presentation skills in front of a new audience. This can range from a simple repeat of a previous presentation you gave before, to a whole new presentation specifically for a situation they've made up. Either way, remaining calm and confident is best first step forward. When you're building your presentation, be sure to practice your talk track with friends or family, or with a professional, so as to ensure that you are smooth in your execution. Even the best presenters and speakers practice their craft; as they say, practice makes perfect—*and* practice makes you prepared, evening out the kinks and allowing you to move slides around or clear out questions before you get in front of the real group.

The Final Interview

You've made it! You've finally done it: you're well on your way to a higher salary, higher benefits, and a position that meets your actual goals in life, instead of one that you *had* to take. Now comes the most crucial step: the final interviews. This is typically another interview with the hiring manager or the hiring manager's boss. Here, they are going to internally conference on you before potentially calling this interview so as to iron out any final details. This could be a weird response to something you said, or it could just be a formality. To get to this step could be anywhere from two weeks to 10 weeks or longer, depending on the company and the need to fill the position.

In this final interview, you want to ensure you're answering the questions as directly as possible. The interviewer is looking for a specific answer; that's why he set up another interview! If you were finished after team interviews, you'd be in official negotiation already. This stage can also come because the company has more than one person they're interested in, so they're trying to finalize who would be best for the position. With this in mind, it's very important to be direct. But how do you compete with an unknown "enemy?" A few tips and tricks:

1. **Restate why you think the position is a great fit.** You should do this based on how your skills align with their needs. This is interview three, four, or five, so you should know what they are looking for by now. Align your skills to directly fill that need.

2. **Reiterate your values.** They may be looking for a cultural fit, and you should be, too.

3. **Ask, "Is there anything else I can clarify for you to help make a swift decision?"** This is a pointed, direct question to your manager. If they are confused or have questions about something, they can ask it at this point. You're being upfront and asking, so it shows your initiative and intention to move forward *(hint, hint, nudge nudge)* with them.

Once you've finished the interview—and any interview, for that matter!—the next steps are key: I like to call it "Wrap It Up", whereby you're sealing the deal and affirming your position on the position. Even if you're rejected for the position—because, let's be honest, not every position is a perfect fit for everyone—, rejection is *normal*—although you should at least get a reply in this case, instead of being left to wonder what happened to the position. You may even get some additional insight to help in your next interview.

CHAPTER 3:
WRAP IT UP

AFTER THE INTERVIEW, DON'T FORGET to send a personalized thank-you email to the recruiter, manager, and anyone else you met during the process; this shows you valued their time, and can also reiterate your skills in a soft way so as to wrap up exactly why you are the best for this position.

An example email would be:

Hello, [ABC],

Thank you again, [ABC], for meeting with me today in regard to the [XYZ] position. I really appreciated our conversation around [XYZ], and believe that my previous experience at [ACBD] would greatly improve/reduce/expedite [situation they're trying to fix that you discussed in your interview]. I look forward to hearing more.

Please do not hesitate to reach out with any questions. I'll follow up with [XYZ (the recruiter/contact person that set the appointment)] at the end of the week to check in if I do not hear anything back.

Regards,
[Your name, email, and phone]

Pro Tip: Do not send the same email to each person you met with, because in all likelihood, they *will* compare them: it's happened to me before! I managed to still get the job, but got asked on the first day if I had sent that email to everyone. Please, learn from my mistakes: don't do it. Just spend the five extra minutes and write custom emails.

Some people ask why I include the last line in the above email template, and the primary reason for this is that you're setting the expectation of what their job is, and making reference to the actionable timeline of decision. This is saying that:

1. Yes, I am valuable;
2. Yes, I am interviewing other places and don't have an infinite amount of time;
3. If I'm not the ideal candidate, let me know so I'm not sitting around waiting forever;
4. It's rude to ghost people, so don't do it, recruiter/possible boss;
5. I'm going to be following up; I care about this position; I appreciate that you're busy, but I deserve respect and the courtesy of a timely reply.

Typically, these emails are very well-received, and, if the interview went well, you'll almost always receive a quick reply from the recruiter and manager. This is normally a good indication of an incoming offer.

And now, the wait begins.

There are really only two outcomes for this situation: they either follow-up and offer you a position, or they don't. However, it's how you respond to both that should matter and can provide you with some insight into how the interview went. Even if you don't get the position, it should still be a learning experience!

At this point, you might want to reflect on the way you have gone about fulfilling these steps, and evaluate whether there is more you perhaps could have done at any of the given steps. Of course, the overall outcome (e.g., whether you get a positive response from your interview or not) will end up indicating this, but some self-reflection for the future can certainly do no harm. The same can be said for additional training and approaches to professional improvement (please see https://beautyandaboss.clickfunnels.com/joinus).

If You Didn't Get An Offer...
Send a follow-up email to the recruiter and manager, thanking them for their time again—and then (and here comes the tricky part) *ask for feedback.*

Some people will not give any, and that's fine; only send one email. However, imagine if you *do* get a valuable piece of constructive criticism. One of the most valuable pieces of feedback I ever received was from a job that I'd really wanted and didn't get into. Their response was:

Thank you so much for following up, Ashley. Although your resume was in line with our expectations and you seem very eager about the position, we believe that we need a more tenured leader in the position to navigate this journey. Please keep us in mind in the future as you progress in your career.

Now, did this sting? Of course.

But at the same time, I obtained great insight from this. I learned that I needed to exemplify my leadership qualities more; that I needed to craft a persona that was older and wiser than my years; and that they were still open to hiring me in the future. Incidentally, two years later, they offered me a position for double the pay, and I declined due to their lack of professional development opportunities—but that's water under the bridge now!

But the lesson in all of this is that, regardless of the outcome of those emails, you should take the opportunity to learn more about yourself. Be self-reflective as often as possible; after all, getting an outside view of yourself (and an honest one, at that!) is extremely difficult to find. Hence, this will help you to prepare for further interviews, and to grow as both a candidate and a person. Remember, when growing, there will be places of struggle; so use these as moments of opportunity to learn! This isn't personal; it's business.

The business of success.

Now, let's switch gears and say all went well: you got the first offer.

Now, it's negotiation time.

CHAPTER 4:
NEGOTIATION TIME

YOU'VE NAILED THE INTERVIEWS, AND the final interview is complete; you've received an email from the HR Manager, stating that the company wants a quick chat. This is normally the time when you'll receive the whole, "Congratulations, we'd like to offer you the position!", which is great—but don't let all your hard work go to waste; the next steps are crucial for completing your transformation and getting that pay rate you deserve!

You've already done the legwork; you know what the salary range is in your market; you know what you expect; and they likely just offered you a set amount of money. Hence, three scenarios come from this:

1. They are way under what you were expecting (greater than a 10% difference);
2. They are over what you' were expecting (10% higher or more);
3. They are within the range you were expecting (plus or minus 10% of what you expected).

Each of these situations should be treated differently for obvious reasons, but remember, you're always negotiating *up*:

even if they gave you more than you expected, there is a chance that your expectations were just too low. Either that, or they *really* needed to hire someone, and you so happened to be the perfect candidate—so always ask for more! Don't miss out on the opportunity to have a truly stellar start.

Before we dive into the offers and how to handle the negotiation, we have to establish a proper understanding of each offer (a.k.a., the Total Compensation Package), especially if you're comparing companies and salaries! You want to make sure you understand all the pieces so that you can fairly evaluate all the positions.

First things first, let's look at the salary. Salary is the easiest number to look at, but don't get overwhelmed by just a higher salary number: it's a great first start and an easy way to quickly compare similar companies, but you want to make sure you also take a look at the other pieces of the puzzle.

Additional compensation items may include:
- 401(k) Match
- Quarterly/Yearly Performance Bonus
- Commission
- Stock or Options
- Retirement or Pension Plan
- Time Off/Sabbatical
- Flexible or Remote Working Environment
- Insurance (Health, Vision, Dental, Life, Disability, etc.)
- Additional Fringe benefits (gym memberships, on-site cafeteria, daycare, eldercare, holiday events, etc.).

Although salary is the easiest to compare, you want to take a look at the Total Compensation Package. In the initial offer, you may not have all the details, but you should certainly know your pay, if insurance is offered, your bonus, stock options, and your time off. Further, when comparing offers, be sure to look for the things that are most important to you (e.g., if you have children and need to be able to drop them/pick them up at daycare, a flexible work schedule may be more valuable than an extra $2,000 in salary).

To evaluate the packages, try and place a dollar value or a comparable numerical value on both offers.

For instance, let's say you received two offers and you're currently a married woman who enjoys travelling and has a small child. Take a look at these two offers:

	Offer 1	Offer 1 Value	Offer 2	Offer 2 Value
Salary	$70,000	$70,000	$85,000	$85,000
Bonus	10%	$7,000	none	–
401(k) Match	5%	$3,500	3%	$2,550
Stock Options	100 shares	$5,000	None	-
Time Off	4 weeks	4 weeks	4 weeks	4 weeks
Flexible Work?	Yes		No	
Insurance	All		All	
Fringe Benefits	Daycare	$5,000	Gym	$240
Total Compensation		$90,500+		$87,790

The shocking piece: Offer 1 actually has a higher value, even though the salary is significantly lower. This is why it's so important to compare offers. It's also important even if there is only one offer, as here, you can understand the true value of the package outside of the salary. In current times, many companies have enormous fringe benefit packages— particularly in the technology and start up fields—, so don't overlook the offers just because there is a lower-than-expected salary! One of the biggest misses that most people forget to look at is the 401(k) Match and the bonus structure, as it's not always listed as a highlight, and can sometimes even be mixed in with the rest of the compensation package. However, it accounts for a lot of money over time, and can even grow as your pay tier/position increases.

Pro Tip: If you look at nothing else, look at the salary, bonus, and 401(K) Match.

So, with all of this in mind, let's take a look at the three situations you could be in with your offer.

Situation One

In Situation One, the offer is way below what you expected. This hopefully won't happen, since one of your leading questions with the HR team was the range for this position. Let's say you were expecting a range between $50,000-$70,000 from HR, but you really wanted $75,000—and then they came in at $50,000. This can certainly happen, especially if you're in a market that has a large supply of interviewees, or if the position you've applied for is very desirable position due to the company benefits. However, this doesn't mean you can't counteroffer and negotiate up! Don't allow the low offer to distract you: you didn't "lose," and you're not a bad interviewer. This is only the beginning. Now is the time to take calculated action to increase your chances of landing the job you want, at the *pay* you want.

You should respond in a way that compliments the offer but directly speaks to your skills and shows your value. You need to *redemonstrate* yourself as an expert. You need to calmly and rationally explain that you want a higher wage. Don't be swayed by the lowball offer; many large companies do this, regardless of how well the interview went; this is because they're trying to save as much money as possible, and most women tend not to negotiate. Why pay you $75,000 when they can pay you $50,000?

A few *don't*s to start with:
- Don't name-call
- Don't say "I'm better than this", or any phrase that contains such a negative connotation
- Don't ask antagonistic questions (e.g., "Why didn't you offer me what we discussed?")
- Don't ask to speak to a manager or bypass the person who is sending you the information; you won't get anywhere if you try to disrupt their process at this point
- Don't get discouraged! Remember, this offer isn't the only offer you can get, and this isn't the only company. If they say no and can't offer you any more money,

then weigh up your options and pass on the opportunity if it's not the right one for you. You hold the final choice, and so be sure you're comfortable and confident in your decision. Don't settle for less than your worth!

Now, let's look at some *do*s:

- Thank your interviewer and the HR person who responded to you
- Use positive language and reinforce that you do want the position
- Acknowledge the offer that was presented to you
- Address any concerns you have with the position, the manager, or the company
- Make a counteroffer!

I've had great luck when I've structured a response in this way:

Thank you, [XYZ], for the offer. I appreciate the time and effort you've taken with me over the last few days/weeks/[amount of time it took]. However, as discussed with the hiring manager and the HR Manager, [my skills] align with a more senior salary in the higher end of the salary band. I'd be happy to hop on a call and discuss further. Please let me know when you're available. I look forward to hearing back and becoming a member of [XYZ Company].

Pro Tip: Don't give the recruiter a price right back in email if this is the first back-and-forth: talk over the phone for this matter, and then you'll be able to *hear* how committed they are to the offer, and how much room there is for negotiation.

When you send a response email framed in this way, it establishes multiple things:

- You're interested in the position (the most important part for them)
- You want to discuss more
- It's not enough pay (a minor fact for the HR person to begin with!).

Remember, they're hoping you *don't* negotiate so that they can get a super employee at a super discounted price. Most companies lowball you to begin with unless it's a super tight labor market; then they don't have that luxury! There is room for negotiation, especially if you carry yourself as a leader. By confirming your interest and demonstrating your value, you're elevating yourself—which, in turn, elevates your expectation and pay. Good for us, this is something companies understand.

One of two things will happen here: you'll either get an email to hop on a phone call; or they'll respond with a simple email asking what your expectations are. With the email drafted above, I've never had someone outright deny me or my clients and come back and say, "No, thank you." *Could* this happen? Sure. But is it unlikely? Yes. Why? Because you didn't outright deny them; you just want to talk about the matter further. HR Managers don't want to lose a great candidate over $1,000, so they'll at least hear you out first.

In the first scenario (where they want to hop on the phone), it's easy: get on the phone, the quicker the better! As my sales brain says, time kills deals! You don't want to allow someone to take your opportunity by waiting a week or two to hop on and negotiate, so the sooner the better. This also keeps your interviews fresh with the manager and HR team, which then makes it easier to remind them of your skills and witty banter.

Now that you're on the phone, it's time to listen more than you speak: you want to get your point across whilst simultaneously getting the HR person to divulge how much wiggle room there is in the budget, since this offer is *far* below what you were expecting. Watch for key language when talking to the recruiter or HR Manager (e.g., "What were you considering?", or, "What is your bottom line?"); this indicates that they are trying to establish what the lowest offer they can make is that you will still accept. *This* is a true negotiation.

To get the negotiation started, thank them for the opportunity and explain that you're excited to discuss the offer in further detail. The HR Manager may jump in and say something along the lines of, "I saw that you said we were drastically below what you were expecting; what were your expectations?"—or, alternatively, they may say nothing. Either way, that's the goal of this call: to move that needle forward. If they don't ask that question, you should. The phrasing should be the same: you should start with the fact that you had discussed salaries earlier, and say the expected range; then, address the salary they gave you with a line like this:

HR Manager, I know when we initially spoke that we discussed a range between fifty and seventy thousand, and I discussed that I'd like to be at least near the high end of that range. However, the offer I received was at the very low end of that range. Was there a reason for such a low offer?

When you phrase your answer in this way, you're re-establishing where you wanted to be and reminding them that you already discussed the salary—so this is really a shock. You also gain clear insight into *why* you were given the salary you were given: in case things with the negotiation don't work out, you may have found a new way to improve your interview skills or resume!

Let's say the HR Manager says the reason was because they don't have anything left in the budget, and the position was for both Senior Manager and Manager roles, and they saw you in the Manager category. This gives you the opportunity to refine your skills, give your years of management experience, and reframe your current position. It could very well have just been a misunderstanding! This is also the time to come back to the HR Manager and give 5% above your bottom line—if you're still actually interested in the position, that is! Since they started you with a bottom-barrel offer and already said they don't have any money in the budget, it's clear they were truly hoping you would just say yes—but you don't want to sacrifice your life for a new job! This may not be the opportunity for you, so set your number and stand strong. If they started you at $50,000 and your bottom line is $60,000 (the range being $50,000-$70,000), I'd counter at $65,000 with the following words:

I understand your position and the reasons for your offer; however, given [x] skills, [y] years of management, and [any information that rebuts their reasons], I really can't accept an offer at less than sixty-five thousand. Do you think this is something that is obtainable? I love the company and know I would be a wonderful addition to it.

The HR Manager will then respond with either, "Let me take this back and I'll let you know", or, "I just don't think that is something we can accomplish." If they say the latter, ask for insight as to the bottom-line salary they could offer. This doesn't mean you have to accept it, but it at least gives you a last chance in the negotiation—and, because you programmed in an additional 5%, there may still be an opportunity to be above your bottom-line price. Remember, you don't ever have to accept an offer: stay firm with your bottom-line price. The whole goal of this entire process is to become a Corporate Queen and to elevate your corporate standing, and taking a job below your worth or out of desperation won't help that. However, also keep in mind that if they *do* counter at your bottom line, it *is* within your range.

This doesn't mean you have to accept it, but it *is* a huge step up from where you were, and does meet your requirements!

So, let's review: they came back at your bottom-line price and then had to talk to the manager and get approval, and he approved!

With just a simple phone call and email, you were able to go from $50,000 to $60,000! That's a 20% increase and $10,000 additional dollars in your pocket this year. Congratulations! This is the power of negotiation.

Even if you landed in the other situation, you gained valuable insight into the reason for the salary, and you move on. Not every offer is going to be a great one, and not every company is going to be a good fit, so don't get discouraged from a lowball offer; onto the next!

Now, let's take a step back and say you weren't in Scenario One, but were actually in Scenario Two—an ideal starting offer!

Scenario Two

Scenario Two and Three are really the ideal spots to be in, since you're already in the ideal price range with your ideal companies. If you start your negotiation in either one of these scenarios, congratulations! You've done a great job up to this point, *and* you're with a company that sees your value. However, don't let that fill your head and let you give up now; you can always reach for more. In Scenario Two, you're within 10% of your ideal salary and total compensation—which certainly means there's still room for improvement! The main difference between Scenario One and Scenario Two is that in this Scenario, you're already where you want to be—and, in most situations, you'd think of just accepting this offer right out of the gate. However, here, you want to tread carefully, as you don't want the offer to disappear, but you *do* want to be sure that you earn your worth! As we've discussed throughout the book, the initial negotiation is the most important stage when it comes to setting up the rest of your career at your new company, so you want to make sure you get the most out of this offer and that you are truly happy with where you're starting.

Let's go through the steps: you've got the initial HR email, so try this template in your response:

HR Manager,

Thank you again for your continued time and effort throughout this process. I'm very pleased to receive this offer and would like to discuss it with you over the phone, as I have a few outstanding questions. Would you have time within the next few days to discuss this with me? I believe this company and position will be a great fit for me, and I'm excited to bring my skills and expertise to [Company Name]. I look forward to hearing from you soon.

[Your Name]

Normally, when you're in this position, the HR Manager is happy to hop on a call and knows what to expect from it, so onto Step 2: the follow-up phone call. When you get on the phone, they're going to ask what your questions are, so feel free to share any that you may have and finish with a simple statement:

Although I appreciate the offer, it is lower than I expected. I expected to be closer to [your true ideal number, or 5% higher than what the current offer is, if it is already near your current offer], as we discussed in my initial interviews. I love the company and know I will be a great addition to it, so how can we make this work?

The HR Manager will normally say; "Let me take this back to the management and see what I can do." This is a great sign: very rarely will they say this and *not* come back with at least a little more, even if it's $1000 ($1,000 more than you would have had!). It's then up to you if you wish to accept or pass on the offer. If, however, they can't do it, and have already given you their best and final, they will typically tell you right on the phone. Be sure to say, "Okay, I need to think about my options. Let me get back to you in a few days." You want to show that you're still interested and are going to weigh up your options. You don't want to lose the opportunity if they truly gave you a fair offer and don't have any room for increase. You want to seriously consider the total compensation package if they cannot increase the salary; they may be more flexible with the bonus, or even the time off or working environment! Remember, a flexible working time or working from home may not have a direct dollar value, but they *definitely* have a life value to many! This is where the third and final step comes in: accepting the offer. At the end of the day, you were already at your ideal salary range (or very close), so all increases are a win! And don't forget: if they accepted your initial counter, that is a full 5% more than what you were expecting—just from a *simple negotiation*. That is the true power of asking for what you want! You don't, however, want to accept a position you don't want, even if it's in your ideal salary range; this is because you still want to confirm the job duties, and that the position is one that will help elevate you to your goals. If you've got all green lights, time to accept! Congratulations!

Now, we've saved the best for last: Scenario Three, where you have been offered a salary above and beyond what was ideal and expected!

Scenario Three

Scenario Three seems like it's too good to be true: an offer over 10% above what you wanted and were expecting! First off, a *huge* Congratulations is due: you really showed your worth in the interview with a company that truly values their employees and doesn't want to lose you. A word of caution to this tale, however: before you reach out to the HR Manager and immediately accept and jump for joy, this is the perfect time to do additional research and make sure your expectations were actually in line with the position. You don't want to lowball yourself or undersell the amount of work the position requires. This can commonly happen when a position is listed as Senior Manager or Manager.

Pro Tip: You don't want to accept the Senior Manager job at a top Manager price; that would be undervaluing yourself and setting yourself up for long-term failure!

Make sure you verify what position the offer is for and what your responsibilities would include; you also want to go back to your job boards and investigation and verify that the specified price is within the range (even if it is at the high end). If you're in a tight job market where employees within your field are tough to find, then this might just be the perfect opportunity; some offers truly are just amazing. Just make sure you check your bases so that there are no nasty surprises!

At this point, you've reviewed the offer and it's legit! You're in the right place at the right time: the company is great, and it's a great total compensation package. One option is to absolutely just accept it: it's clear that you've have shown your worth in the interview, that the company values your and its employees, and it is more than you hoped for; hence, all the signs indicate that you're setting yourself up for a great position with continued advancement. However, there is always the opportunity to ask for more: if you're truly well-qualified and a true perfect fit, the company won't want to risk losing you. The difference with *this* conversation is that the tone needs to be imminently positive so that the HR person doesn't pull the offer or give it to someone else. Although rare, this does happen with stellar companies that get lots of job applicants, so you want to be prepared. Any time you're negotiating, there is risk, but you've got to risk it for the biscuit!

A good framework for this email will cover the following items, and be very similar to Scenario Two:

- You're appreciative of their time and effort
- You appreciate the offer
- You absolutely are interested and want the job
- You'd like to negotiate the offer.

Similarly to Scenario Two, you can ask the HR Manager for a quick call to go over the details and finalize any questions you have. After you've gone through your initial questions, be firm but friendly and ask about the salary or the fringe benefits. Again, in this scenario, 5% is a standard negotiation range, so whatever the offer you received was, you can add 5% to that salary and negotiate from there with the HR Manager and team. It's crucial that you confirm your interest in the position, even if there is no room for an increase, as you don't want to lose the position—but don't come from a place of fear! You're worth the extra 5% and deserve it, and with an initial offer as high as this one, the company may absolutely agree with you. Be sure to state your qualifications and fall back on your connections and integrations during your interviews. With such a high offer, an increase is actually more likely; it's a confirmation that the company really wants you and has had trouble finding the right candidate. Typically, the HR Manager will take your new offer back to the team and discuss, and with a little bit of luck, you'll have got it!

Congratulations on not only increasing your salary from your current position, but also on going above and beyond with your new offer. You've made more than 10% over your last position, you're at a better company that appreciates you, and you've set yourself up as a leader for your new position for increased success in the coming years!

Regardless of the position you're in, you've made huge strides toward your new goals and becoming a Corporate Queen! Regardless of whether you fall into Scenario One, Two, or Three, you're now aware of the full total compensation package and have a better view of exactly what you want—and how to get it! You don't ever have to accept a position that you hate, or stay at a job that doesn't allow you to grow to your fullest potential, ever again.

If you haven't found the right job yet, keep looking! It's just a click and an interview away. You never know what opportunity can be right around the corner, so always keep your eyes open. Remember those non-negotiables and keep looking!

SECTION 3:
THE AFTER-EFFECT

CHAPTER 1:
I GOT THE RAISE/NEW JOB!
NOW WHAT?

WELL, FIRST, CONGRATULATIONS! LOOK AT you go! You've shown your strengths and proven that you *deserve* to be paid your worth and live your Corporate Queen life!

But now what?

You've started in your new position, but you don't want to rest on your laurels and get comfortable: you've got a plan to be a superstar, and you need to maintain that image when you start at your new position. The easiest way to set yourself up for continued success is to set boundaries and goals from the onset (and, of course, that ever-pressing need to absorb as much additional learning and training as you can, as available at https://beautyandaboss.clickfunnels.com/joinus).

The Secret to Success: The Performance Plan
Now that you're a Badass B*tch and running your game, you've got to have a plan to stay on top. Since you've

conveniently just negotiated a raise or started at a new job, you need to set ground rules and boundaries for development.

The first thing that I recommend is formulating a performance plan—a plan between you and your management that describes, in detail, what your responsibilities are, what the acceptable behavior is, and what exceptional behavior is. The exceptional part is crucial: if you're in there killing it every day, you should be rewarded! If you're putting in the work, you need to have a plan for progression in payment and job level.

In the corporate world, it's very common to have a yearly performance review. When you're starting at your new position, be sure to ask what the performance review process looks like so that you and your manager have a clear understanding. In this initial meeting, you should also discuss how pay increases work, if performance bonuses are given (and what the qualifications are), and the timing of performance reviews.

I know this can be daunting; after all, you just *met* your boss and negotiated that 10% raise! However, remember that you are worthy. Don't forget, you work to live, not live to work. Employees are the biggest assets to their employers, especially with unemployment as low at it is, and it's becoming increasingly difficult to find and keep good workers. Hence, asking about performance reviews upfront sets the standard that you (and your time) are valuable: you're showing your confidence in exceeding expectations; you're demonstrating that your skill and hard work should not go unnoticed; and you're demonstrating that you will not stay around to be mistreated.

I've found this to be a hard concept for most women to understand; they're so nervous to talk to their new boss about a performance review for their fear of being fired, or of coming across as confrontational. However, I dare you to look at this differently:

- Is asking how you will be "graded" at work confrontational, or really just a level-set for both parties?
- Is setting a standard from the beginning of work so that both sides understand the expectations rude?
- Does setting the measurable goals that are associated with pay hurt how you will perform at work?

No, no, no! Measurable goals and expectations don't hurt how you will perform; they *increase* performance. Standards don't cause inequality; they exemplify *excellence*! Goals tied to pay don't cause you to work less; they *motivate* you to work smarter, because now you actually have a viable incentive!

In your performance review, you should ask pointed, specific questions, such as:

- How is my raise determined? When are raises given? Who determines if I receive a raise?
- What are my goals for the next 90 days? Next year? How do these tie into the team/corporate/group goals?
- What is my stretch goal(s)? What would you consider to be exceptional performance?

- Let's talk about my career path; what would be possible career roles as I grow and develop in my current role?
- How can I help you to reach our team goals?
- How can I develop my skills further in [growth area]?
- Can we set up a check-in meeting in 90 days to ensure I am on the right path and that my goals still align with the company and team focus?
- Could you introduce me to other managers and people in the areas in which I am trying to grow? I'd really like to learn from anyone who is willing to teach!

These last four questions are often music to employers' ears: they are so incredibly important, as they show not only that you are focused on raising yourself up, but that you are focused on raising the company and your team. You're a true team player and are trying to gain skills—not to leave, but to improve the company! Typically, questions of this nature tend to lead to conversations with leadership: you're showing the initiative that you want to become your very best. You don't just want to get by, and *that* is where real negotiating power comes in. You're in this for the long run, and the company would be foolish to lose someone who is that dedicated (and they know it!).

Now, I know this can be daunting; you're literally setting yourself up for improvement. But that is what this is all about: you're here to succeed, not just to get by! You're setting standards to get paid, but that also means you have to hold up your end of the bargain—so no skating by. When you're direct with your employer, they tend to be direct back.

With this style of negotiation, you're saying, "I am here; I am worthy; I have value; I deserve more; and you should pay me in paper." However, by that same token, you're also saying, "I will work harder; I will be open to feedback; I will grow as an employee; I am loyal; and I want you to help me to help you."

These are power statements, and when you're direct in your negotiations, you get what you want—but you also have to mean what you say. You need to be present and give your best self every day; you need to show up to win. There is no breezing by unnoticed.

The whole point of this process is to be noticed, because if you got this raise, that means you *really* want the next one! You're worth it: you got management attention and you got the job, so now show them what you're worth and make sure you're rewarded for it! Don't get complacent: keep on your toes, and hold your employer to the same standard. If performance review time comes around and it gets put off or breezed over (which can certainly happen, especially if bosses/the work climate changes), make sure you mention it! Bring it to the attention of the boss above yours; bring it to the attention of HR. Don't suffer because of corporate bureaucracy—and, if those strategies don't work, look for another position.

Go back to Chapter 1 and start again. You're not this job; you're a collection of skills, experience, personality, and adventure. You're an asset to any employer who understands the value of you as an employee. You can find a career and a position that is fulfilling and supports your goals.

Remember, you deserve everything you want and more. Don't ever settle for less, and if you can't find it, create it! You'll never regret it. And, if one day you decide that maybe corporate just isn't for you and entrepreneurship is your new path, reach out, and I'll get you started on the path to success!

Yours in sass and class,
Ashley

www.ingramcontent.com/pod-product-compliance
Lightning Source LLC
Chambersburg PA
CBHW071558200326
41519CB00021BB/6800